FASHION MODEL

FASHION MODEL

a career guide

Gay Search

*In association with the
London Academy of Modelling*

New Bond Books
Weidenfeld and Nicolson
London

Contents

Photographic acknowledgements

The author, the London Academy of Modelling and the publisher are grateful to the following for their kind permission to reproduce the illustrations: headsheet and index card, *People in Pictures*; Shirley Anne and Josephine Florent, *Honey magazine*; fashion shows, *Gregg and Bailey*; David Warbeck and Philo, *Barrie Knitwear, photographer Francis Loney*; Tricia, *photographer Swapan Mukerji*; making a television commercial, *Great Guns Ltd*; 'before and after' make-up and hairstyle shots, *photographer Bill Ling*; *Vogue* cover, *Condé Nast Publications Ltd, photographer Barry Lategan*; Twiggy, and location: the tropics, *Vogue magazine* (*Condé Nast Publications Ltd*); model on beach, photographed in Tobago, *Vogue magazine* (*Condé Nast Publications Ltd*), *photographer Norman Parkinson*; all other photographs, except the example of modern cosmetic dentistry, *Mike Montgomery*.

Foreword

Grateful thanks to all those busy people in the world of fashion and beauty who gave me the benefit of their time and experience. Without them, this book would be considerably thinner.

Gay Search
London, 1976

Introduction

Undoubtedly, the model girl was the folk heroine of the sixties – the female equivalent of those working-class pop stars, hairdressers, footballers and photographers who ousted the debs and the chinless wonders from the gossip columns and from the driving seats of Rolls Royces, and who enabled *Time* magazine to saddle London with that dreadful 'swinging' label. And, as with so many cult figures, the image of the model girl so overshadowed the reality that many of the girls themselves were no longer sure where one ended and the other began. Films like Antonioni's *Blow Up* helped to cement the image of the permissive, self-seeking amateur without much brain, and the Press only compounded the felony. For a long time, any pop singer's girlfriend, with no other claim to fame, or any girl involved in a scandal became a 'model' for the purposes of the story. And it was the myth that the public were presented with, while the reality, which was much the same as it had been when models were first invented, remained a mystery.

Ever since the nineteenth century, when *haute couture* came within the reach of an ever-growing number of *nouveau riche* women and was no longer reserved for royalty and a handful of titled ladies, couturiers have needed girls to show – and sell – their clothes. In the early days, models were on the same level as the most menial seamstress, and were looked on simply as mobile clothes horses, whose looks and personalities were of no importance whatsoever. They were even dressed in bizarre, long-sleeved, high-necked black satin garments under the outfits they were modelling, so that their bare arms or shoulders wouldn't distract the audience's attention from the clothes.

From the twenties onward, couturiers began to choose their models for their looks as well as their figures, but it wasn't until the fifties that girls like the almost legendary Fiona Campbell-Walter and Barbara Goalen made modelling not only a perfectly respectable career, but also a rather glamorous and desirable one. In those days there was only a comparatively small number of top models, elegant, sophisticated, beautiful women who did every type of work – couturier's shows, shows for the big stores, and the rather limited amount of photographic work available at the time.

But then, in the sixties, the fashion industry exploded. Suddenly London's boutiques were leading the world in young fashion, and every girl, whether she was an heiress or a shorthand typist, could afford to buy clothes by the new fashion *élite* – Mary Quant, Foale and Tuffin, Biba, Ossie Clark. Fashion was young, fashion was fun, and fashion was for everybody, and it needed a whole new breed of models to show it off to advantage – young, sexy, dolly girls who looked like the girls you'd see in the King's Road on a Saturday morning, not the aloof, unapproachable women who filled the pages of *Vogue, Harpers* and *Queen.*

Magazines sprang up, catering to this new market – *Honey, Petticoat, 19* – and even the established ones began to demand a new style of fashion photography, and a new style of modelling – fluid, energetic, exciting. David Bailey, it's often been said, was the first photographer to make models look sexy. He disagrees. 'I think I made them look natural. Most photographers were homosexual in those days, and I think I brought a man's view of women for the first time, which is how women like to see themselves.' It was Bailey, of course, who played a large part in the creation of the first modelling superstar, Jean Shrimpton, whose face became as familiar to most people as any film star's. She travelled all over the world to exotic locations, was photographed *with* all the right people *by* all the right people, had only to sneeze, practically, to be front page news, made an awful lot of money – and suddenly every girl wanted to be a model.

The appeal was obvious. You didn't need good connections, it didn't matter who your parents were or where you went to school, you didn't need an array of O-levels, you didn't even need talent. All you needed was the right face, the right figure, an ability to 'project' in front of a camera – an instinctive, rather than an acquired skill – and within a matter of months you could be rich and famous.

For one girl, anyway, that was true. Less than a year after she left school, seventeen-year-old Lesley Hornby from Neasden was famous all over the world as Twiggy. Girls from New York to Tokyo tried to look like her, bought the clothes and tights marketed under her name, shop-window dummies were created in her image, and her name became synonymous with thinness in many a music-hall comedian's jokes. Now, in her mid-twenties, she has established herself as a film and television star, although again it's her personality, which helped her get to the top as a model, rather than her acting, singing or dancing ability, which has been the secret of her success. No doubt about it, Twiggy was lucky in being born with an extremely photogenic face and the ability to respond to a camera, and she did get some lucky breaks – such as being called 'the Face of '66' by the *Daily Express* only weeks after she'd started out on her career – but it wasn't only luck that took her to the top. Other girls have been labelled 'the Face of '69' or ''71', and their names have long since been forgotten. Twiggy had an extremely astute manager in Justin de Villeneuve, who knew how to make the most of the breaks she did get, and Twiggy herself worked very hard at her career, always keeping one step ahead of fashion and changing her image when the time was right.

But for the majority of girls, the rags-to-riches-overnight story is simply a fairy tale. As the seventies have proved now that all the furore of the sixties has died away, modelling is an extremely demanding, full-time job that requires stamina, determination, an uncrushable will to succeed, and sheer hard work. It wouldn't be putting it too strongly to say that, these days, if you want to get to the top, you must be prepared to look on modelling as a vocation. The competition is so fierce and the standards so high that unless you are prepared to put your career above everything, you won't get to the top.

If you have a date one evening and the photographer you're working with wants to work late, your date will have to go by the board if you ever want to work for that photographer again. You may adore potatoes, but they are fattening so you must cut them out of your diet. If your friends are going on to a late-night party, but you've got a booking next morning at nine, and if you don't get eight hours' sleep don't look your best, then they'll have to go on to the party without you. A busy model simply cannot afford to lead the kind of social life the newspapers would have you believe that all models lead. Nobody is going to book you again if you arrive late for a session and with dark circles under your eyes, because you didn't get to bed till three the night before.

But no matter how hard the realities of a model girl's way of life are stressed, most people still think it is one of the most glamorous careers of all – the kind of job most teenagers dream about and which gives their mothers nightmares. But it shouldn't, because these days modelling can be a very viable, rewarding career for a girl. If she is interested in fashion and has the right physical requirements, then a job as a house model in a whole-sale fashion house, where she'd also be expected to carry out some office work, would give her much more satisfaction than a secretarial job in a solicitor's office or a bank. It can also be an excellent grounding for a career in fashion as a showroom manageress or a buyer, a journalist or a public relations officer.

A lot of girls who have the right physical qualifications never consider modelling as a career, because they look at photographs in *Vogue* and *Harpers* and think they couldn't even begin to compete with the models they see, forgetting that high fashion photography is merely the tip of the modelling iceberg. But it would be misleading to suggest that any girl who wants to be a model badly enough can do it. There are certain basic physical requirements for which even the prettiest face is no substitute. For fashion modelling, you must be at least 5′ 6″ (there are a few jobs for the smaller girl, modelling petite ranges, but only a very few), have a size 10 or size 12 figure, and longish legs. Even a perfect hour-glass shape won't make you a model if your legs are short and fat. For photographic work, particularly advertising, height isn't so important, though obviously if you're very small the work you can do will be very limited.

It's impossible to be specific about faces, except to say that most top models have good bone structure – high cheek-bones and a small, neat nose – big eyes and a generous mouth. Of course, there is a fashion in faces, but it's up to you to create it. Nobody wanted short, bobbed hair and eyes made huge by drawn-in, spidery lashes until Twiggy came along, and the oriental look wasn't all the rage before Marie Helvin.

It's very difficult to be objective about yourself, and even more difficult for your nearest and dearest to be objective about you, so if you want an honest, unbiased opinion of your chances of success as a model, ask the people who ought to know, such as the top model agencies. They are seeing potential models all day long, and they know whether you're likely to get work or not. Even if they like you, they are unlikely to be very flattering or to take you on, on the spot. They will probably suggest that you enrol at a reputable model school, and a fairly reliable guide to reputability is the fact that the best schools have their own licensed agency attached, and will guarantee either to put you on their own books when you have finished your training, or to help you find a suitable alternative. Cherry Marshall and Lucie Clayton both have good reputations, as does the biggest school in London, the London Academy of Modelling.

Before you can enrol at the London Academy, you will have an interview with a member of the staff – many of whom were top models themselves – including an interview in front of a television camera, which will be recorded on videotape and played back to you. Your height and measurements will be taken and you'll be given an honest assessment of your chances of making it as a model. Of course, their verdict needn't necessarily be right – almost everybody in the fashion business has turned down girls who've gone on to become very successful models – but since they also have an associated model agency and are aware of the cold, hard commercial facts, they can assess your chances of making a living fairly accurately.

If you're told that it's unlikely you'll be successful as a model, there is no reason why you shouldn't still take the course and benefit from it. Nobody would claim that learning how to apply make-up skilfully or how to enter a room properly is the instant passport to success, either socially or in your work, but it can be a great help in boosting your self-confidence, and helping you to make the most of what you've got, which can, in turn, lead to professional and social success.

If you're told that you do have the makings of a model, you might wonder whether in that case you need to take a course at all. Admittedly, any girl can become a model – you don't need any professional qualifications to enter the business. But without training you have to learn the hard way, if – and these days it's a very big 'if' – you can find someone who's prepared to give you a chance. You do sometimes hear about girls being spotted by photographers in boutiques and starting their careers that way, but the vast majority of girls start their working life in wholesale fashion houses, and with so many trained girls to choose from, they're unlikely to take on a girl with no training.

At the London Academy, you will learn how to walk properly on a catwalk, how to turn, how to show all types of clothes to their best advantage, how to respond to a television camera – even if you never make a television commercial in your life, the chance to see yourself as others see you is invaluable – and how to apply a really professional model make-up. You'll be given lectures on hair care, skin care, diet, exercise and on what is expected of you as a model from the people you'll be working with, such as agents and photographers – everything that a would-be model needs to know.

For teenagers, older women and men, the London Academy runs separate courses which cover all the relevant basics, and the areas in which their training and career prospects differ from the girls'. But the essentials for success are the same for all models. Anyone who is prepared to work hard, to be totally professional about everything they do, and who has the right physical requirements, can build a financially rewarding and very enjoyable career, with opportunities to travel and to meet creative, interesting people.

There is always a demand for new faces, and there is always room at the top.

1 Deportment

The most important asset a good model can have is not her face, or even her figure, but the way she moves. Whether you're modelling clothes in an *haute couture* salon in Paris or in a small wholesale showroom in the 'rag trade' district of London, the customers aren't going to be looking primarily at your face, they're going to be concentrating on the clothes you're showing, and the way you move – how you present that coat or that pair of trousers – can make all the difference between a non-committal 'Um, quite nice' and an enthusiastic 'Oh yes!' backed up with a firm order.

In general, good show models are made, not born – no girl can get on to a catwalk for the first time and stand, walk, and show clothes, like a professional model. Obviously if you're naturally graceful, if you walk well, and your body responds instinctively to music, then you're half-way there, but a model's walk isn't a natural walk – it's something that has to be learnt. Ten or fifteen years ago, it was possible for a girl with the right figure to land a modelling job without any training and to learn the tricks of the trade by watching her colleagues and from her own mistakes, but these days modelling is much more fiercely competitive than it was, and how many employers would take a chance with an untrained girl when there are half a dozen trained ones to choose from?

If you've set your heart on a photographic modelling career, you might think that learning deportment is a waste of time, but you'd be wrong. For one thing, only a handful of girls go straight into careers as exclusively photographic models, and when they do, the money they earn can take as long as six months to come through, so it's extremely useful to be able to do the occasional fashion show or 'season' to earn some ready cash. And for another thing, photographic modelling isn't simply a matter of standing in front of the camera like a statue while the photographer works miracles around you. He'll want you to be able to move, to use your body expressively, and learning to walk on a catwalk in front of other people is the first stage in losing that self-consciousness which makes you stiff and awkward in front of a camera, and in becoming aware of your own body and what it will do.

When you start learning how to walk like a model, you must try and forget how you usually walk. You're no longer striding down the High Street, arms swinging briskly – you should be gliding along the catwalk as though you were literally treading on air.

But before you even take your first step, you must know how to stand properly. Starting at the top, your head should be straight, with your chin parallel to the floor, your shoulders should be back, both your stomach and your bottom pulled in, your hands relaxed by your sides, your right leg slightly forward, with the knee bent, and your right foot turned slightly outwards, with the heel in line with the arch of your left foot.

Now, keeping all that in mind, start to walk, leading off with your front – right – foot, and moving from the top of your hip bones instead of from the tops of your legs as you usually do. It isn't difficult once you've grasped the principle, and the easiest way to get it right is to hold your stomach in, push your pelvis slightly forward and keep your bottom tucked in tight – try and imagine you've got a solid gold pencil between your buttocks which you must, at all costs, keep in position! Normally you walk by putting your heel down first, and then your toe, but when you're modelling, you put your toe down first, then your heel. At first, it feels very unnatural – like learning to walk all over again, so it helps to exaggerate the movement and point your toe like a ballet dancer before it touches the ground until you get used to it. Try, too, to keep your feet pointing straight in front of you, though if they must deviate slightly from the norm, then it's better for them to point out-wards than inwards.

When you're learning to model, the right shoes are essential. A simple court shoe with a two-and-a-half inch heel and no platform is ideal – a lower heel makes walking smoothly more difficult, a higher heel throws your weight too far forward, and a platform, particularly those huge orthopaedic-looking ones, make it impossible for you to bend your foot, essential when you're trying to learn the 'toe-heel' movement.

As with anything, the only way to perfect your walk is practice. The more you do it, the smoother and more natural your walk will become, and you'll find too, that you're much lighter and quieter on your feet.

Ideally, the top half of your body, from the waist up, shouldn't move at all – you shouldn't sway from side to side or bounce up and down. Every-thing about the way you move should seem so smooth and effortless that, if you were wearing a long dress, your audience might easily imagine you had wheels instead of feet. When you're walking in your natural way you swing your arms, but, since that causes a great deal of movement in the top half of your body, when you're modelling you should barely move them at all. Try to keep your hands very close to your sides, and if you feel you *must* swing your arms, then make sure that it's no more than a few inches backwards and forwards. If your hands feel awkward just dangling by your sides, then try pressing your thumb against your ring finger – it gives you something to do with your hands so you aren't so conscious of them, and makes them look a little less like a frozen plaice, too.

In the fifties and sixties, it was fashionable for models to use their hands a good deal, to draw attention to various details on the garment they were showing, but these days the style of modelling is much simpler, much less fussy. Once you've finished your training and are working as a model, then you can use your hands if you want to – you can slide your fingers in the top of a patch pocket on a jacket, say, provided you don't shove your hand too far and push the whole garment out of shape – but while you're learning it's best to use them as little as possible. Otherwise what tends to happen is that girls get carried away with the idea and wave their hands around like tic-tac men.

Once you've begun to master the model walk, you'll need to know how to do a half turn. As you're walking along the catwalk, step on to the toe of your right foot, then pushing yourself lightly round with your left foot, turn through a semi-circle and finish up with your feet at 'ten to two', your left foot slightly behind your right, with the right heel in line with the left toes.

If you're working in a salon or at a fashion show where there is a stage forming a T-shape with the catwalk, you'll need to know the threequarter turn to get smoothly from one to the other. If you're turning to the left, then, as you step off the catwalk, you take a step to the *right* with your right foot, already beginning to turn your body in that direction. Then, using your right toe as a pivot, take a step with your left foot and push yourself lightly round until you're facing the left-hand side of the stage, with your feet in the same position as they were after a half turn, ready to move off with your right foot. If you're going to the right, then you turn to the left and use your right foot to spin yourself round. It might seem an elaborate way of getting from A to B, but simply turning left or right looks very clumsy. It takes a little time to grasp the threequarter turn, mainly because you're turning in the opposite direction from the one in which you want to go, and at first you'll find yourself hesitating at the top of the catwalk while you work it out in your head, but, like riding a bicycle, once you've mastered it you'll never forget how to do it.

The other turn you'll need to know is the full turn. When you're modelling along the catwalk, as you bring your right foot forward, go up on to the balls of your feet, then, using your right toe as a pivot, turn your body to the right. When your *left* shoulder is pointing along the catwalk in the direction in which you were originally going, bring your left foot across, slightly to the side and in front of the right one, keeping both feet close together. Then, still using your right toe as a pivot, push yourself round until your body is facing the front again. Now move off, starting, as always, with your right foot. At first you'll find that your full turns are a bit wobbly or creaky, but with practice you'll find them becoming so smooth and natural that you won't even have to think about what you're actually doing any more.

When you're modelling you'll find that you're using all the various turns in different combinations – if you're modelling in a wholesale house or a small fashion show, then you'll work out your own routine, but these days all the top fashion shows have a producer, or even a choreographer, who'll plot it all for you if the routines are dance routines rather than straight modelling ones.

Once you've learnt the basic techniques of modelling, you'll move on to the refinements. Since clothes reflect different moods, different settings, even different personalities, obviously the way you model them must reflect these differences too. Even in everyday life you don't feel, or behave, the same in jeans and a T-shirt as you do in long, floaty evening dresses. When you're modelling trousers, you can afford to be a bit more boyish – your walk can be more like your normal walk, though it's probably best to stick to a modified 'toe-heel' model walk at first to make sure you don't get carried away and stomp along the catwalk like a storm trooper. You'll still do half turns, but full turns would look rather silly, so instead, when you reach the middle of the catwalk, you bring your right leg across in front of you, pivoting on your left toe at the same time, so that you come to rest facing the audience on the left-hand side of the catwalk, feet astride, legs straight, showing the line of the trousers. You hold that pose for a moment or two, then, pivoting on your left toe and stepping with your right foot, turn to the left, so that you wind up in a similar pose, facing the other side. Pause again, then continue your walk with your right foot down the catwalk. With trousers, the back view is as important as the front, if not more so, so it's all right in this instance to turn your back on the audience.

If you want to emphasize the boyishness of the pose, you can put your hands on your hips – or rather rest your clenched fists lightly on your hip-bone, making sure that your wrists are lower than your knuckles.

If full turns are wasted on trousers, then they're essential to show off long, full evening dresses. You can also emphasize the fullness of a long skirt by bringing your knees up higher as you walk – this pushes the fabric out in front of you and creates more movement in the skirt, which is always very attractive.

Evening wear, like casual clothes, brings out the actress in a good model. If the dress you're showing is a very demure Victorian style, then you could try modelling it like a modest Victorian miss, with your hands linked in front of you, and your eyes shyly lowered. If the dress is skin-tight, backless and slashed to the navel, then you must really vamp it up and make Shirley Bassey look like Ena Sharples. In practical terms, full turns are not only unnecessary with tight dresses, they're also very tricky, so rather than risk winding up in the audience's laps, settle for two half turns instead. If you're modelling a coat and dress, then, as you get about half-way down the catwalk, begin to unbutton the coat, using only your left hand, and without looking down. It's really very easy – you slide the fingers of your left hand under the flap of the coat, keeping your thumb on top, then, when you come to the bottom button, raise the fabric slightly with your index finger and push the button through the hole with your thumb. Move on to the next button and undo that in the same way. When all the buttons are undone, you can either push the coat back out of the way by putting your hands on your hips to show the dress underneath, or you can take the coat off.

If it's a heavy coat, take hold of the lapels and lift it clear of your shoulders. Let your arms drop slightly behind you so that the coat can slide freely down them and when you feel your hands coming clear of the sleeves, take hold of the coat with your right hand in the middle of the collar, bring it round to the front, and fold it neatly over your left arm so that none of the lining is showing.

If you're modelling a light coat or jacket that won't slide easily down your arms, lift it clear of your shoulders as before, then, with your arms behind you, take hold of the left sleeve in your right hand and pull it free of your left arm. Still holding on to the left sleeve, bring your right arm, and the coat, round to the front, then with your left hand take hold of both sleeves and pull the garment free of your right arm, too. Again, with your right hand, take hold of the coat in the middle of the collar and fold it over your left arm.

If you're modelling a fur coat, slip it down your arms behind you, take hold of the centre of the collar and drag it nonchalantly along the catwalk behind you.

It's rare in fashion shows to find girls modelling on their own – there will usually be at least two of you, often more, on the stage and catwalk at the same time. In that case, either the director of the show will tell you what to do, or else you can plan your routine together beforehand. In both cases, it is important to keep together – to keep in step, to turn at the same time and the same way, both inwards, or both outwards, but not one each way.

So far we've been dealing mainly with fashion shows and *haute couture* salons where there are almost always catwalks, but in most wholesale fashion houses, where most show models start their careers, you simply model the clothes on the showroom floor. Most of the basic techniques are the same – the walk, the turns, the way you model trousers and coats – but the way you present the clothes is different. In a large showroom, you model each outfit to every buyer or group of buyers sitting at tables all round the room. You usually model towards them and away from them, rarely from side to side across their line of vision.

In a smaller showroom, you'll model the outfit in the centre of the room, then move quickly round to the individual buyers or groups of buyers to let them have a closer look at the dress or coat, but you don't model it as extensively each time. In most wholesale houses, you'll be expected to quote the price of the garment you're modelling and possibly the style number too.

Of course, it's important to master all the techniques that a show model needs so that they become second nature, but you could be absolutely perfect technically, and still not be a really good show model. What you must always remember is that you're not a mobile tailor's dummy – you're selling to your audience, and that involves projecting your personality. If they like you, then they're more likely to like what you're wearing.

At first, of course, you'll be nervous, and the last thing you'll feel like doing is smiling at anybody, but you must force yourself to smile, even if you do feel frozen-faced and silly. It's a cliché, but it happens to be true – if you smile at people, in nine cases out of ten they'll smile back at you. Look at your audience as you walk down the catwalk, pick out individual faces and look them in the eye. Remember that they're already on your side – if they're an audience at a fashion show, they've come to enjoy themselves, and if they're buyers, they're out to do a successful day's business, so they certainly aren't hoping that you're going to make a fool of yourself by tripping over your feet and falling off the catwalk. Remember, too, that you're a model from the moment you arrive at work to the moment you leave. Even if you're not actually working, don't slouch around chewing gum or sprawl on chairs – you never know who might see you. And when you're modelling with two or three other girls, don't think that because one of them is actually showing her outfit just then, nobody is looking at you so it doesn't matter if you stand staring vacantly into space. Be interested in what's going on, and, above all else, smile.

Very few models find that they really don't like modelling to a live audience once they've overcome their initial shyness. The majority come to love fashion shows in particular, and thoroughly enjoy the response of the audience and, of course, the applause. After all, there aren't many jobs where you get that kind of appreciation.

2 Diet and exercise

For some people food is a source of great pleasure, while for others it's merely fuel, to be taken on board two or three times a day, or comfort, a consolation for the deficiencies in our lives, but for most models it's calories, and their major concern is what effect it will have on their waistlines.

Of course, if you're modelling, your weight is crucial – if you get a job as a house model with a firm that needs a size 12, and you put on two inches all over, then no matter how good you are, or how much they like you, you will almost certainly lose your job, and although one or two fashion editors are prepared to let out zips or work behind-the-scenes miracles with safety pins if they really like your looks, the majority will thank you for coming, and book another girl who can actually get into the clothes.

But if you're a busy, working model, you cannot afford to ignore the fact that food is essential fuel, and that what you eat will show, one way or another, in your nails, your hair, your eyes, your skin. And don't forget, modelling is extremely hard work and you'll need all the stamina and energy you can get, so tempting though it may be to skip breakfast and simply grab a sandwich at lunch-time, you do so at your peril – from the point of view of both your health and your beauty.

To stay healthy, your body needs regular intakes of protein, fat, carbohydrates, vitamins and certain minerals, all of which a sensible, balanced diet will give you, without your having to take handfuls of vitamin pills every day. (Vitamins are good for you, but your body can only absorb a certain amount – usually what a well-balanced diet will give you – and any excess just goes to waste.)

You should try and ensure that, every day, you eat some meat or fish, some eggs, cheese, butter and milk – they'll give you lots of protein, some fat, an assortment of vitamins and some minerals, such as calcium, essential for strong, healthy bones and teeth – some fresh fruit and vegetables, eaten raw if possible, since cooking removes a large proportion of the vitamins they contain and reduces their effectiveness as roughage, which you need to prevent constipation. You should also eat some bread – provided, of course, it's wholemeal bread and not the white, processed variety which does little more than fill a gap – as it's a rich source of protein, vitamins and roughage.

You should try and cut out sugar altogether – all the starch you eat, for example bread and potatoes, is broken down into sugar by your body, and along with natural sugars, such as fructose which is found in fruit, should provide as much as you need for energy. Processed sugar, both brown and white, is not only very bad for your teeth, it's also extremely fattening – most food substances in the body perform vital functions like repairing tissues and replacing cells as well as providing energy, but sugar does nothing but provide energy, so any excess is turned immediately into fat.

It's probably no coincidence that the foods you need to keep you healthy – meat, fish, eggs, cheese, milk, fresh fruit and vegetables – are also the foods that will help to keep you slim, but the fact that there are around five million overweight people in this country suggests that far too many of us are stocking up on what the Americans call 'junk' foods – the cakes, the biscuits, the beans on toast, the bars of chocolate – which not only fail to provide your body with the calibre of fuel it needs, but also make you fat.

It is, as Professor Yudkin, the nutritionist, points out, difficult to pin down who is fat and who isn't, especially when we're talking about ourselves – 'I am well-built, you are overweight, she is fat!' Those charts which give 'average' weights according to height and build are of some use, but really only if you are considerably overweight. For instance, if you're 5′ 7″, then according to the charts – and even they vary slightly – you should weigh something between 9 st 7 lb and 10 st 11 lb, depending on whether you have a small, medium or large frame, but you could weigh 10 st 8 lb and, in spite of your big bones, still be overweight.

The only real way to tell whether you could afford to lose a few pounds is to look at yourself, without the rose-coloured spectacles, in front of a full-length mirror. Is there a hint of a spare tyre round your waist? Can you take a generous pinch of flesh between your thumb and forefinger? If you lie flat on the floor, can you place a ruler down your side so that it touches your ribs and your hips, and nothing in between? If you can't, then you're overweight. Before you get down to the business of slimming, though, it's worth knowing why you are overweight, and in almost every case, the nutritionists tell us, the answer is simple – you're taking in more fuel (food) than your body is burning up as energy and what's left over is being stored as fat.

Of course there are exceptions, but it's surprising how often that simple statement is true. Being overweight makes most people feel rather guilty and so, rather than admit that they eat too much, they'll come up with any

Calorie chart

If you decide to diet by counting calories then you will find the following chart very helpful, but do use it sensibly and make sure yours is a balanced diet. A bowl of cream of tomato soup, a packet of crisps and a Danish pastry would be within your limit of 900 calories, but you wouldn't be able to eat anything else that day and your hair, skin and general health would suffer.

DAILY CALORIES FOR QUICK WEIGHT LOSS

MAN moderately active	1,700
MAN sedentary	1,400
WOMAN moderately active	900
WOMAN sedentary	700

	Weight	Calories		Weight	Calories
Dairy produce			Ham, boiled	4 oz	250
Butter	½ oz	110	Hamburger	1 med	125
Camembert	1 oz	90	Kidneys, grilled	4 oz	120
Cheddar	1 oz	130	Lamb, chop grilled	4 oz	310
Cream cheese	1 oz	230	Lamb, roast	4 oz	330
Dutch cheese	1 oz	90	Liver, grilled	4 oz	180
Cottage cheese	1 oz	30	Pork, chop	4 oz	400
Egg, fried or			Sausages, beef	2 oz	140
scrambled	2 oz	135	Sausages, pork	2 oz	165
Egg, poached or			Turkey, roast	4 oz	200
boiled	2 oz	80			
Margarine	½ oz	110	**Fish**		
Milk, fresh	½ pt	190	Cod, baked	4 oz	95
Yoghourt, plain	1 oz	25	Cod, grilled	4 oz	95
			Haddock, smoked		
Meat and poultry			or poached	4 oz	115
Bacon, grilled	2 oz	185	Herring, grilled	4 oz	190
Bacon, fat grilled	2 oz	350	Kipper, grilled	2 oz	100
Bacon, gammon	2 oz	520	Mackerel, grilled	4 oz	200
Beef, corned	4 oz	280	Plaice, steamed	4 oz	100
Beef, roast	4 oz	255	Sardines, tinned	2 oz	160
Beef, steak	4 oz	330	Salmon, tinned	4 oz	160
Chicken, boiled	4 oz	220	Shrimps, fresh	2 oz	55
Chicken, roast	4 oz	200	Sole, steamed	4 oz	90
Frankfurters	2 oz	144	Tuna, tinned	4 oz	280

	Weight	Calories
Drinks		
Beer, mild bitter	½ pt	80
Bovril	1 cup	4
Cider	¼ pt	120
Chocolate with milk	1 cup	180
Coffee, black	1 cup	5
Coffee, white	1 cup	38
Cola drinks	1 glass	80
Gin	single	57
Lager	½ pt	120
Orange juice	1 glass	50
Scotch	single	57
Stout	½ pt	100
Tea, milk and sugar	1 cup	50
Tea, black	1 cup	20
Tomato juice	1 glass	30
Tonic, slim line	1 glass	1
Biscuits, bread, cereals		
All-Bran	1 oz	88
Biscuits and cake	1 oz	140
Bread, brown	1 slice	51
Bread, white	1 slice	51
Slimcea	1 slice	32
Chocolate biscuits	1 oz	145
Cornflakes	1 oz	105
Porridge	1 oz	13
Vegetables		
Baked beans, tinned	2 oz	50
Beetroot, boiled	2 oz	15
Brussels, boiled	4 oz	20
Cabbage, boiled	4 oz	10
Carrots, boiled	2 oz	10
Cauliflower	4 oz	10
Celery, raw	4 oz	10
Cucumber	2 oz	5
Lettuce	2 oz	5
Mushrooms, grilled	2 oz	18
Onions, boiled	4 oz	15
Peas, fresh	4 oz	70
Peas, tinned	4 oz	95
Potatoes, boiled	4 oz	90

	Weight	Calories
Potatoes, crisps	2 oz	320
Runner beans, boiled	4 oz	8
Spinach, boiled	4 oz	30
Tomatoes, fresh	2 oz	10
Fruits		
Apple, baked	1 large	100
Apple, fresh	1 med	40
Apricots, dried	1 oz	52
Apricots, tinned	4 oz	100
Banana	1 med	50
Cherries, fresh	4 oz	45
Currants	1 oz	69
Dates	1 oz	70
Figs, dried	2 oz	122
Figs, fresh	1 oz	12
Grapefruit, half	3 oz	18
Grapes, fresh	4 oz	60
Melon	4 oz	30
Orange, fresh	4 oz	40
Peach, fresh	3 oz	30
Pears, fresh	4 oz	50
Pears, tinned	6 oz	110
Pineapple, fresh	4 oz	50
Pineapple, tinned	6 oz	120
Plums, fresh	3½ oz	40
Prunes, stewed	2 oz	60
Raspberries, fresh	4 oz	25
Raisins	1 oz	70
Strawberries, fresh	4 oz	30
Sultanas	1 oz	69
Miscellaneous		
Gravy, thick	1 tbsp	35
Honey	1 spoon	14
Ice-cream	2 oz	110
Jam	1 spoon	13
Pastry	1 oz	163
Soup, clear	1 bowl	32
Soup, creamed	1 bowl	200
Spaghetti in sauce	4 oz	70
Sugar	½ oz	55
Syrup	1 spoon	15
Treacle, black	1 spoon	13
Yorkshire pudding	4 oz	250

number of excuses. Some will tell you they're overweight because their bodies retain water or salt. If that is true, then they should see a doctor, because it's only when you're suffering from certain illnesses that your body retains more fluid or more salt than it needs. If you're healthy, then your body regulates very carefully how much of each it retains – if you have too much fluid, your body gets rid of it through the usual channels, and if you have too little, you feel thirsty and so take in more. Some women, admittedly, do find that they retain fluid – and so seem to put on weight – in the few days leading up to a period, but both revert to normal when the period actually starts.

It's very rare for people to have too little salt in their systems, but it can happen if you're in a very hot climate and sweat profusely, and the result is usually a very unpleasant cramp. Most of us take in about ten times as much salt as our bodies need, but, provided we're healthy, we dispose of the excess with no trouble at all.

Other overweight people blame their 'glands' for their condition, but, as Professor Yudkin says in his excellent book *This Slimming Business*, the only glands that cause overweight are your salivary glands! In a few cases, a deficient thyroid gland can be the cause of the problem, but since it carries a number of other side-effects, your doctor would know at once if that was the problem in your case.

Another popular, often-heard excuse for overweight is heredity, but again, in almost every case, it *is* only an excuse. If both your parents are overweight, then it's easy to think that you've inherited their physique, but it's much more likely that you've inherited their bad eating habits. Admittedly, if you've been brought up from birth to consume vast amounts of food, then it is difficult to get into good eating habits when you reach your teens and become very self-conscious about your size, but in the long run it's the only way to get slim and, more important, to stay slim.

The part of your brain that controls your appetite is called the appestat, and when it's working properly it ensures that you eat enough to give you the energy you need, but no more. Obviously, since so many people are overweight, not everybody's appestat does work perfectly – it's a very delicate mechanism and can be affected by so many outside factors, such as getting into bad eating habits as a baby, being ill or unhappy – and if yours is one of them, then you need to retrain it, which takes will-power and time.

Open any woman's magazine or newspaper and chances are that you'll see some new wonder-diet, guaranteed to take pounds off you in a matter of days. It may be very effective in the short run, but it's more than likely that you'll have put all that weight back on again in a matter of weeks. Doesn't it make more sense to aim to lose four or five pounds over a month or six weeks that will stay lost, than to lose in a week six pounds which you'll have put back on again before the month is out?

Crash diets are never a good idea if you want to lose weight permanently – for one thing they are so strict that it would be bad for your health to stay on them for more than a few days, and it takes weeks, even months, for your appestat to get used to less food, and therefore to want less. And for another, you get so hungry on most crash diets that, when you stop, you'll eat too much and put back everything you've struggled to lose. It seems pointless to be miserable on carrot juice and lettuce leaves for three days, if you're only going to go back to your usual diet of hamburgers and chips and bars of chocolate when you've finished.

The same is true of the vast array of slimmers' aids on the market now – soups, biscuits, even chocolate bars – because you couldn't spend the rest of your life eating two slimmers' biscuits and a glass of milk at every meal. Apart from the health aspect, the monotony would drive you mad, and if you only stay on them for a few days at a time, you'll probably revert to your bad old weight-gaining ways when you stop. Anyway, the majority of slimmers' meals are based on sweet things, like biscuits, and one of the most important elements in retraining your appestat is to wean yourself away from sweet, starchy foods.

The only artificial aids that can be of real benefit to slimmers are saccharine as a substitute for sugar – beware of glucose, sorbitol or honey, since they have as many calories as sugar, and there is no scientific evidence to back up the extravagant claims made for honey by its supporters – and starch-reduced bread or crispbread. It must be starch-reduced, though – any other so-called slimmers' bread or crispbread is as fattening, weight for weight, as the real thing.

In spite of a growing awareness of good dietary sense in this country, there are still a surprising number of 'fad' diets that appear from time to time. There was the milk and banana diet, and the hard-boiled egg diet, which was supposed to work on the principle that you used more calories in digesting the eggs than they actually created, so that they were giving you 'negative calories' – a theory totally without foundation.

More recently there was the grapefruit diet in which it was alleged the acid from the grapefruit 'burned up' the fat – another theory without any foundation in the truth. But the grapefruit diet did contain some good sense. For one thing, it started off by listing all the foods you *had to* eat, before it listed the many more foods that were banned, which was a great psychological boost, and for another, it was basically a very rigorous low carbohydrate diet.

This diet, which allows you as much meat, fish, cheese, eggs, butter, milk, even cream, as you like, since these foods contain no carbohydrates, plus almost unlimited amounts of green vegetables, which contain almost none, and a very carefully controlled amount of bread, cake, rice, pasta and so on, is very popular with nutritionists at the moment for several reasons – first, because it's well-balanced, second, because there's an enormous variety of things to choose from, so you're unlikely to get bored and relapse into your old ways, and thirdly, because it's very easy to live with – you can go and eat at friends' or in a restaurant and have whatever's going, provided, of course, you give the bread, potatoes and pudding a miss, without feeling deprived and without upsetting your hostess.

Basically the low carbohydrate diet is the same as counting calories, except that, instead of having thousands of units to deal with, you have only about ten, since only carbohydrate-containing food counts – which is much easier for people who aren't too good at maths.

Another advantage of this particular diet for both health and weight is that, although in theory you're allowed as much fat as you like, in practice you'll find that you've cut down your intake of that, too. As you're not eating bread or potatoes, there's nothing to spread butter on, and as you're not eating cakes or biscuits or pastry, you're not taking fat in that way, either.

Although one of the pluses with this diet is that you can follow perfectly normal eating patterns, it is even more effective if you nibble throughout the day – keeping within your allowance, of course – rather than eat just one or two main meals. The reason is that, every time you eat, your digestive system comes into operation, and since that requires energy to function, it's burning up fuel which would otherwise be converted into fat.

It isn't a good idea to go without breakfast – if you do, both your body and your brain will begin to flag around midday, whether you notice it or not, and you're more likely to indulge in a mid-morning biscuit with your coffee – a large part of your daily carbohydrate allowance. You shouldn't leave your evening meal till late either, since your system needs time to cope with the influx of calories before you go to bed, and nutritionist Derek Miller has found recently that gentle exercise after a meal does help increase the number of calories your digestive system burns up. Exercise in general, though, plays only a small part in controlling your weight. It is true that the more active you are, the more energy you burn up so that there's less to be turned into fat, but exercise alone isn't a means of slimming. Professor Yudkin has worked out that you'd need to walk from London to Brighton to burn off one pound of fat, and your appetite would be so stimulated when you'd finished that you'd probably eat too much and replace that pound in one go.

What exercise *can* do for your figure, though, is firm up your muscles and get rid of any flab so that although your weight stays the same, you are actually slimmer. With the right exercises, it is possible to go down as much as a whole size in trousers without losing a pound.

But, like eating sensibly, there isn't much point in exercising unless you're prepared to do it regularly. Muscles need constant use to keep them firm and it's surprising how quickly they revert to flab once you stop. From the health point of view, exercise is essential – your heart and lungs need to work flat out at least once a day – and the fact that you feel better when you've done it isn't merely psychological either. When you exercise hard, your body produces adrenalin, its own built-in pep-pill, so that for a while afterwards you do actually feel just a little bit 'high'.

You might like to get your exercise through sport – tennis, squash, athletics are all good in moderation, but perhaps swimming, which tones up the muscles in your neck, shoulders, bust, arms, stomach, thighs, calves and feet, is the best of all. Skipping is good, too, because you can do it in a confined space, or you could take up cycling – an ideal way of getting round London in the traffic and of keeping your thighs and calves in trim at the same time. You shouldn't do too much horse-riding, though, since it tends to over-develop your thigh muscles. It's not a problem for most work, but it would probably rule you out for swimwear or corsetry. In fact, one leading photographer, when he's auditioning girls for bikini shots, always asks them whether they ride or not. If the answer is yes, he doesn't even bother to see them in a swimsuit because he knows their thighs will be too muscular.

If you're not the sporty type, then you should try and get into the habit of doing ten or fifteen minutes exercise every day, either when you get up – a marvellous way to get your circulation going and make you feel wide-awake – or before you go to bed, when, funnily enough, it seems to have the opposite effect and can help you sleep.

Work out a routine for yourself – preferably to music, since the rhythm is an incentive to throw yourself into it, and it's more enjoyable – that includes some general loosening-up exercises, plus some for specific parts of your body, your bust, for instance, or your stomach, or your thighs. Don't neglect your bottom, either – it's surprising how many girls who otherwise take great care of their bodies, do. According to one of the judges in last year's Miss World competition, many of the girls lost marks because their bottoms were flabby.

There are so many different methods of exercise to choose from – yoga, which can be of great benefit mentally too, modern ballet, isometrics – that you'd be wise to attend some of the multitude of different classes held in

London and in other big towns, to find out which suits you best. Anyway, when you're starting, classes are a good idea because the other girls give you moral support, and unless you're very strong-willed, you're not likely to push yourself just that little bit harder if you're exercising by yourself at home.

So, by eating sensibly and by keeping your body in good shape, you'll not only reap the benefits now in terms of a near-perfect figure, and all the stamina and energy you need to cope with a busy modelling career, but you'll still be looking good at fifty.

3 Teeth

A lovely smile is an asset to any girl, but to a model, a photographic model especially, it's absolutely essential. Just glance at the piles of magazines on any bookstand – apart from one or two of the glossies, like *Harpers*, *Queen* and *Vogue*, whose covers do feature a cold haughty stare sometimes, almost all the other women's magazines, from *Hi!* to *Woman's Own*, feature a big wide smile. Although naturally smooth, soft, well made-up lips do help, the most important ingredient in your smile is your teeth. Every model should have teeth she can be proud of – not simply for the sake of appearance, but also because they play an important part in building up her self-confidence. The girl who feels that her teeth are ugly is much more reluctant to smile and often talks in a way that hides her teeth, which makes her come across, in an interview for example, as a rather quiet, down-beat, even dull sort of girl, which she probably isn't.

Almost any dentist will tell you that, with a few exceptions which we'll deal with later, the best teeth you can have are your own, and provided that you look after them properly, they should last you a lifetime. But it's a very big 'provided that' – the fact that around twenty-nine thousand teeth are extracted *every day* in this country is a very clear indication that very few of us do look after our teeth properly.

The root of the trouble is that most of us have got our attitude to our teeth all wrong. We believe that the health of our teeth is largely the dentist's responsibility, not ours, and we think of dental care as going along to the dentist twice a year, having our teeth scaled or filled or pulled out, but very few of us ever think about *preventing* the decay that makes all the restoration work necessary.

'It's essential that patients realize how much they can do for themselves,' says a leading West End dentist. 'I see them perhaps two days a year on average, and on those days I can make sure that their teeth are really clean and free of decay but if they're going to neglect them on the other three hundred and sixty-three days, then nothing I can do will be of any real use.'

In people under twenty-five, decay of the crown – the visible, white part of the tooth – is the major cause of lost teeth, while among the over twenty-fives it's peridontal disease – disease of the gums and the roots of the teeth – that's usually to blame. But in both cases the basic problem is the same. It's the combination of sugar with dental plaque – the substance made of millions of bacteria which coats your teeth – that does the damage, and, quite simply, if you can eliminate one of those two things, you won't have any more dental disease.

Although dental floss (a special fine thread for removing food particles from between your teeth), wood points, even sophisticated gadgets like a water pick, have their uses, basically you remove dental plaque by brushing your teeth properly – and again, 'properly' is the operative word.

'There is no one correct way to brush your teeth,' says the dentist, 'and no correct number of times. If your teeth are free of plaque, even if you clean them with an old twig you picked up in the park, then you're brushing them properly. If they aren't, then even if you're brushing them forty times a day with the most expensive electric toothbrush and the newest technique, then you're still not doing it properly. Whether or not you use toothpaste makes not the slightest difference to the cleanness of your teeth – all it does is make your mouth taste nicer and your breath sweeter, nothing more.'

Toothbrushing, he believes, is a skill that can only be taught by demonstration. 'I could spend twenty minutes describing to you how you should do it, but you still wouldn't be any the wiser, and yet that's how most dentists still teach it. Next time you go and see yours, ask him to *show* you – if he won't, then perhaps you should find another dentist.'

One very simple way to find out whether you are getting the dental plaque off your teeth is to ask your dentist for some disclosing tablets, or, if you live near a large, well-stocked chemist, buy some there. Once you've brushed your teeth, chew a tablet and the harmless vegetable dye it contains will stain the plaque red or blue, so that you can see very clearly where you haven't brushed properly – where the teeth join is one of the favourite places, and where they meet your gums. You then brush them again, and only by removing all the plaque will you get rid of the dye, so that when there's no trace of red or blue left on your teeth anywhere, you'll know they are free of plaque.

If you follow that routine for a few days, you'll begin to know how and where you need to brush to get rid of the stained plaque and you'll begin to develop good brushing habits.

In theory, if you managed to keep your teeth plaque-free, you could eat all the sugar you liked with no ill-effects, since it's the reaction of one substance on the other that causes the problems. But in practice, since even the most conscientious of brushers can only remove about ninety per cent of the plaque, sugar is still potentially dangerous.

The dentist again: 'What happens is that sugar combines with the plaque on your teeth to produce lactic acid and that's what dissolves the enamel on your teeth. The amount of sugar you eat is irrelevant. What matters is the number of "exposures" – occasions on which you eat sugar – because there is twenty minutes of acid production for every single exposure to sugar.'

Take a typical girl's day – although not, hopefully, a model's day. Up in the morning with a cup of tea sweetened with sugar, followed by cereal with sugar, or toast and marmalade made with sugar; coffee with sugar, and a biscuit mid-morning, and perhaps a Polo around twelve. Fruit yogurt with sugar at lunch-time, tea and another biscuit in the afternoon, apple pie and custard, both made with sugar, for supper, a few chocolates while she's watching the television, and perhaps a mug of Bournvita, made with sugar, before bed.

That is nine exposures to sugar in the course of one day – a minimum of three hours' acid production, three hours during which the enamel on your teeth is under heavy attack. The solution here is either to cut out sugar in its manufactured form altogether – the natural sugars, like fructose in fruit, are much much less harmful – or limit the number of exposures and try to brush your teeth after each one. Although tooth decay is a serious problem, many dentists believe that it isn't as serious as peridontal disease, caused by the poisons given off by plaque, attacking the gums and the roots of your teeth. 'I believe,' the dentist says, 'that the least important dental tissues are, first, the enamel because I can replace it with gold or porcelain or plastic, and, secondly, the pulp, which most people call 'the nerve', because even if it is removed, I can still restore teeth to their natural function. On the other hand, if the peridontal ligament – the tissue that holds the tooth into the jaw – is destroyed, there is nothing I can do except fit dentures, but, given a sound root in a sound bone, I can build castles!'

The 'castles' the dentist is referring to are crowns and bridges. Crowning, which is usually done on front teeth where the normal silver filling would look unsightly, involves filing the tooth down to a point and cementing a hollow 'jacket' made of gold and porcelain or plastic on to what's left. If the tooth is very badly decayed, then it will be filed completely away, and the jacket will be cemented to a gold 'post' fixed into the root.

Bridging is usually done to fill a gap left by an extracted tooth, and the two teeth on either side of the gap are used to support a replacement for it. Those two teeth are prepared as they would be for crowning, only instead of individual crowns, a unit of three joined 'teeth' is fitted to cover them both, and the gap.

So far we've looked at how to keep your own teeth healthy and what can be done to salvage them if they aren't. A lot of the same techniques of cosmetic dentistry can be used on teeth that are perfectly healthy, but not very attractive. In general terms, the way your front teeth look now depends largely on whether or not you had good dental care as a child. If your teeth were overcrowded when they came through, then a good dentist would have extracted a couple to give the others room to spread. If your teeth were crooked or stuck out, then a good dentist would have fitted you with a brace to pull them back into shape, before the teeth and the bones had really begun to 'set'. If you didn't get that kind of treatment as a child, then you may well need cosmetic dentistry as an adult.

If your teeth are overcrowded, then it's still possible to solve the problem by removing one or two, to give the others more room, or if the degree of overcrowding is only slight, then it's possible to have all the teeth crowned, making each one marginally smaller, but, as the dentist points out, you can only reduce the size so much before it would start looking silly. 'I must say, though,' the dentist added, 'that in some cases overcrowding can look very attractive. Ali McGraw's left front tooth overlaps her right, and she hasn't done too badly with that dental anomaly!'

If your teeth are crooked or protruding, then it's still possible up to the age of about thirty to push them back into place, but of course it takes much longer than it would have done when you were a child, and not many twenty-year-olds, especially if they're models, are prepared to wear braces on their teeth for two years. Again, perhaps the best solution is to have the offending teeth crowned.

It's supposed to be lucky to have gaps between your teeth, but no photographic model would agree with that. A gap between your two front teeth is the exception – look at Patti Boyd! – but gaps all round are a real problem, as they show up black in photographs and look really very unattractive. If they're only small gaps, it's possible to crown them, but again, they can only vary very slightly in size from your natural teeth before they start to look silly. Perhaps the best solution to this problem, for a model, is to get your dentist to make you a slip-on plastic overlay for your front teeth. It just clips on to your own teeth and, since it's moulded in one piece, there are no gaps, and any irregularity in your natural teeth can be eliminated in the plastic ones. It doesn't have any effect on your own teeth at all, and though it isn't designed to eat its way through a five-course meal, it's ideal for photographic sessions.

The other reason for crowning strong, healthy teeth is their colour. If your teeth are yellow, then there is nothing you can do to alter that fact – no toothpaste, no matter what the commercials say, can actually make your teeth whiter – so if the colour does bother you, the only answer is to have the teeth crowned. 'No dentist really likes filing down perfectly strong, healthy teeth in order to put crowns on them, but if it means the difference between a girl having a successful modelling career or not, then I don't believe I should say no. After all, dentists should be treating people, not merely teeth, and if a girl's teeth are making her unhappy, then it's my job to help her.'

You can get crowns done on the National Health Service, but only if they are essential – to replace a decayed front tooth, for instance. If you want your teeth crowned for strictly cosmetic reasons, then you'll have to pay for them yourself. Cosmetic dentistry can be expensive – a single crown can cost between £40 and £100, although the price isn't by any means an infallible guide as to how good the work will be – but it is an investment that will last you a lifetime and could well pay handsome dividends. Don't forget, a surprising number of those lovely smiles that gleam up at you from the covers of magazines are only there thanks to the skill of one of the model's best friends – her dentist.

4 Hair

Any girl's hair is, or should be, her crowning glory, but if you're modelling, then it's another absolutely vital part of your stock-in-trade. Just think what the short, angular bob that Leonard devised for Twiggy when she was just starting out did for her career! Your hair is probably the most important single factor in establishing your image – long and straight for the girl-next-door, a mass of curls for the zany madcap, a simple chignon for the elegant, sophisticated woman – and the more versatile you can learn to be with your hair, the better, but it can also be a real asset in its own right. Glance through any woman's magazine and count the number of adverts for shampoos, colourants and other hair-care products, all featuring girls with immaculate hair. If you've got outstandingly beautiful hair, then you'll never be short of work, even if your face isn't particularly photogenic – a lot of those photographs and the blow-ups you see in hairdressers' windows are taken from the back or from the side, showing only a small part of the model's face, so that all the attention is drawn to her hair.

Like bone structure or skin type, the sort of hair you have is determined largely by luck – if both your parents have dark, very curly hair, it's unlikely that you'll wind up with long, straight blonde locks – but even if you are one of the lucky ones, you'll have to work at it if you want your hair to stay really beautiful, and if you're making the sort of demands on it that every model has to make – frequent washing and blow-drying into shape, setting on heated rollers and so on – then you'll need to be doubly careful.

Leonard, whose staff are responsible for most top models' hairstyles these days, believes that the three most important factors in keeping your hair looking really good are the three Cs – conditioning, cut and colouring. Although your hairdresser does have a part to play in keeping your hair in good condition, it's mainly your own responsibility. For a start, hair is a very sensitive barometer of your general health – if you've ever been in bed with 'flu for a couple of days you'll know how lank and greasy your hair becomes – so for it to be in good condition, it's essential that you are, too.

A sensible diet is a must – plenty of first-class protein like fish, meat, eggs and cheese, lots of fruit and fresh green vegetables, and no greasy or highly spiced foods – and so are fresh air, exercise and enough sleep.

Since the papilla – the minute bud under the surface of your skin from which the hair grows – is fed by your bloodstream, your hair reacts very directly to what is in your blood, and certain drugs, like barbiturate sleeping tablets, will affect its condition quite noticeably.

As a general rule, you should treat your hair as gently as you can, since anything in excess can do it harm. At one time, vigorous brushing was supposed to be good for your hair and scalp, but all it does is stimulate the sebaceous glands – the glands in your scalp which produce oil – which will make your hair greasier, and may well tear or stretch it, too. Always brush gently. Never just drag a brush straight through your hair – start at the back and work your way carefully, section by section round to the front. The best brush for the job, so Clifford Stafford, one of the artistic directors at Leonard, believes, is the denman brush, the kind with a flat back and nylon bristles. On the whole, natural bristle is better for your hair than nylon, since it is softer and so less likely to tear the hair, but for general brushing it's a bit too soft and doesn't get through the hair efficiently. If yours is a blow-dry style, a long bob for example, you'll need a round bristle brush to turn the ends under, and if it's a very curly style you'll find an assortment of Franson brushes – small, round bristle brushes in various sizes – indispensable. The best type of comb to use is one with widely spaced saw-cut teeth, made of bone, horn or tortoise-shell, and not the cheaper nylon or, worse, metal ones, which again can damage your hair.

When you're washing your hair, handle it with more care than usual, since it's much more likely to stretch and lose the elasticity that gives it its bounce when it's wet. Don't scrub away at it, or wring it out as though it were the washing. Before you start, brush it all gently forward from the nape of your neck to remove any dust or dead hairs, then with *lukewarm* water – never hot, as too much heat can damage your hair – wet it thoroughly all over. It's worth investing in one of those rubber shower attachments that fits over the taps, since it makes the operation much easier. For the first wash you don't need much shampoo, as you're only removing the superficial dirt, so measure about a dessertspoonful – less if it's a concentrated shampoo – into your hands, then spread it lightly over your hair. There's no need to work up masses of lather, and anyway it isn't a good idea to dig your fingers too vigorously into your scalp as you'll only stimulate the sebaceous glands and make your hair greasy.

Once you've rinsed your hair and shampooed it a second time, then make sure the final rinse is really thorough, so that your hair squeaks when you pull your thumb and finger along a strand. Trichologists – experts in the medical and scientific aspects of hair-care – stress how important proper rinsing is. 'Any traces of shampoo that you leave behind will clog the hair and make it lank and dull. I'm afraid that the worst culprits here tend to be hairdressers – usually the clients' hair is shampooed by a junior and not enough attention is paid to the final rinse.'

Your choice of shampoo is important – and extremely difficult. The vast range on display in every chemist, all making different claims, is enough to baffle anyone. But in general you should look for a shampoo with a *low* detergent content. Almost all shampoos contain some detergent because it's essential for dissolving grease and dirt, but since too much of it can damage your hair by splitting or flaking the cuticle – the hard, outer layer of the hair, made up of thousands of tiny transparent scales that overlap each other like the tiles on a roof – the less you expose your hair to it the better. On the whole, the cheaper the shampoo, the higher the detergent content, but unfortunately that doesn't mean that every highly priced shampoo in a fancy bottle is automatically low in detergent. Your best bet is to stick to the shampoo used on you by your hairdresser – Leonard, for example, makes up shampoos individually for his clients – or to those made by well-known specialist hair-care firms. After all, their reputation is at stake, so they're not likely to risk putting a bad product on the market. Stephen Way, another leading London hairdresser, recommends using a shampoo designed for overbleached or damaged hair until you find the shampoo which is perfect for your hair, because it is the mildest on the market and can't possibly do any harm. Recently, shampoos with 'natural' ingredients such as essential oils and herbs have become very popular, and they can be good for your hair, but beware of what is basically neat detergent with the odd few herbs thrown in.

At every price – and quality – level, though, you'll find different shampoos for different types of hair. 'Always judge your hair by the condition of the ends, not the roots,' says Stephen Way. 'If your scalp is greasy and the ends dry, then use a shampoo for dry hair.' Shampoo for dry hair tends to be the mildest, since too much detergent would only make the hair still drier, and the shampoo for greasy hair the strongest, but if your hair is *very* dry or *very* greasy, then a shampoo alone probably isn't enough to solve the problem, and you should seek your hairdresser's advice. Dry hair can be treated with a variety of essential oils such as rosemary and eucalyptus which improve the condition of your scalp too, but steer clear of olive oil – for one thing it isn't particularly good for your hair, and for another it is so difficult to get out afterwards that any good it may have done will be cancelled out by all the extra shampoo you'll have had to use.

In the case of greasy hair, the trichologist usually recommends a sensible, low-fat diet, practical precautions such as not using hot water to wash it and not brushing it too much, and a lotion to apply to the scalp. 'We can't alter the patient's physical make-up, we can't stop her being prone to very greasy hair, but at least we can keep it under control.'

Black girls have special hair problems – they tend to suffer from dry scalps and brittle, splitting ends, and the fact that their hair is often so curly that it's a real effort even to get a wide-toothed comb through the tangles, makes the problem worse. There are special products on the market, but since they're mostly imported from America they tend to be rather expensive and available only in areas where there are large immigrant communities, such as Shepherds Bush and Brixton in London, and Handsworth in Birmingham. If you can't get hold of them, the best alternative is to use a good scalp lotion and conditioner.

If you suffer from dandruff, you shouldn't try and treat it yourself. There are shampoos on the market that will keep it at bay, but if you use them for any length of time, you'll find your hair becoming either dull and lifeless or very oily, and so you'll need to buy yet another preparation to counteract those problems. 'If you suffer badly from dandruff,' says the trichologist, 'you should get medical advice, because it can be caused by a variety of different things, some of which are simply to do with your scalp, but others are symptoms of an illness.'

Once your hair is washed, it will almost certainly need conditioning. Conditioners are usually wax-based products which fill in any gaps in the cuticle of the hair and smooth down all the tiny transparent scales so that the hair doesn't tangle and you won't tear it when you pull a comb through it. The fact that each hair is perfectly smooth means that, when it's dry, the light reflects off it and makes it shine. Conditioners can't harm your hair in the way cheap shampoos can, but even so, you shouldn't use them indiscriminately. If you have dry ends but oily roots, then don't apply conditioner all over your head – just put it on the ends where it's needed.

When you've finally rinsed your hair, *blot* it dry in a towel, don't rub it or wring it too vigorously, as you're liable to stretch it. For the same reason, you shouldn't brush it when it's wet either – just comb it carefully through with a wide-toothed comb.

Ideally, you should let your hair dry naturally, but since no busy model can afford that sort of time, you'll have to resort to artificial aids. Never dry your hair in front of a fire, real, gas, or electric, since fierce, direct heat can not only dry it out, it can also scorch it. If you use a hairdryer – a professional salon hand-dryer like the Wigotaifun is probably your best bet, since you'll be using it more often than the average girl uses hers, but, of the cheaper domestic dryers, Moulinex are very good – make sure you don't hold it too close to your hair, and if yours is a simple blow-dry style, then don't pull the hair too tightly round the brush or, again, you will stretch it.

If you set your hair on rollers, then use the foam rubber or wire-mesh covered kind – the spiky plastic ones can tear your hair – and don't wind them too tightly. Almost inevitably when you're modelling, you'll find yourself using heated rollers constantly – a couple of times a day, even, if you have to change your hairstyle in the middle of a photographic session – but although all the hair-care experts agree that they don't do your hair any good, provided you're careful, they needn't do it much harm. If you've got long hair, you need to be extra careful, not so much because the heat dries out the ends and makes them split, but because the ends get tangled round the spikes on the rollers and you'll tear them, trying to get them free. Wrapping a tissue round the roller before you start helps prevent that happening, but the best solution is to have your hair trimmed regularly every five or six weeks before the ends have the chance to split too far. (It's the only cure for split ends incidentally – no shampoo, regardless of what the commercials claim, can 'mend' a split end.)

So cut – the other big C – is essential, not only for the look of your hair, but for its condition. Hair is like a plant – if you let it go on growing without ever cutting it back, it will become thin and straggly. If you've got long hair, next time you have it trimmed ask your hairdresser to show you a section he's just cut off – you'll see that it's much thicker in texture and quantity where he's just cut it than it is at the ends.

Cutting doesn't actually encourage your hair to grow, but since the hair grows more slowly if the ends are split, by cutting them off you allow it to grow more vigorously again. Clifford Stafford remembers Twiggy coming to Leonard before she started modelling, with shoulder-length hair that was 'split up to her ears! We had no alternative but to cut it all off. Now, she's grown it again, and because she's had it trimmed regularly, it's in beautiful condition. In a case like that, you have to go backwards before you can go forwards.'

Twiggy made a friend of Leonard, and any top model will tell you it pays handsome dividends to be on really good terms with your hairdresser. Shop around till you find someone you like and trust, then stick to him, or her, and follow him anywhere. That way, he gets to know you and your hair, and knows what suits you, so he'll always try to send you away looking your best. If you go to a different hairdresser every time, you'll be simply another head of hair to be set or cut, and though he will do a professional job, it won't be anything special, and may not be right for you.

If you're thinking of changing your hairstyle, then do ask your hairdresser's advice, and listen to it. After all, he knows your face and your hair, and can be quite objective about what will suit you and what won't. And no top hairdresser is going to risk his reputation by talking you into having the latest style, whether it suits you or not, just because he's dying to try it out on somebody. 'You must cut hair in a style that is balanced,' says Stephan Way, 'that goes not only with the girl's face but with her height, weight, even the texture of her skin. If the style and the cut are right, then the hair will always look good. If the cut is bad and the style wrong, then even the most skilful setting around won't make it look right.'

When you're deciding on a basic style, you should take into account the type of hair you have. If it's thick and straight, then go for a style that makes the most of it, and the same is true if it's curly. After all, the idea of a good haircut is to make life easier for you, so that if you're constantly having to back-comb your hair or put it in rollers to get it looking right, it rather defeats the object.

But if you decide that you don't like your long straight hair, and want soft waves or a mass of curls, then you can always have it permed, but *don't* try and do it yourself. The chemicals used in perming alter the structure of your hair and so need very careful, professional handling. 'There are so many ways in which home perms can go wrong,' says the trichologist, who spends a lot of his time sorting out the resulting hair problems, 'and the damage you can do takes, literally, months to put right.' But perming is perfectly safe, provided it's done by a professional on strong, healthy hair. At Leonard, for example, you have to see the trichologist before they'll perm your hair, to make sure that it is strong enough, and if you've had your hair permanently tinted, it's extremely unlikely that they'll agree to do it. 'Tinting also alters the structure of your hair, and it can only take so much at a time!'

Leonard's stylists are extremely reluctant to straighten hair. 'It's about the worst thing you can do to it,' says Clifford Stafford, 'not only are you using chemicals that alter its structure, you're also stretching it at the same time to get the curl out, and if you pull it the wrong way at the roots while you're doing it, the hair can break off. I don't like the look of straightened hair, either – you take all the movement out of it, and it just looks lank and dead.'

Until recently, a lot of black girls had their hair straightened, either with strong chemicals or with a 'hot comb', both of which were ruinous for its condition, but now, having realized that black *is* beautiful, most of them are leaving their hair naturally curly and having it cut reasonably short – the Afro isn't really suitable for modelling because it makes you look rather top heavy.

It's hard to improve on superbly cut hair in first-class condition – unless you think the colour is rather dull and you'd like to liven it up. Again, don't try and do it yourself – go to a colouring expert like Daniel Galvin at Leonard, who's recognized as one of the best in the world.

There are three basic types of colouring. First, there are water rinses, which just coat the outside of the cuticle and last only from one shampoo to the next. These days, top hairdressers are using natural colourings like henna, marigold flowers and saffron, which not only give a 'lift' to your natural colour, but are also extremely good for the condition of your hair. Then there are the semi-permanent colours, which penetrate the cuticle of the hair but wash out over five or six shampoos, and the permanent tints which take the natural colour out of the cortex – the core of your hair – and replace it with the shade you've chosen. Think very carefully before you have your hair permanently tinted, because if you don't like it, there's nothing you can do till it grows out.

Daniel will not bleach hair, partly because it's very bad for its condition, and partly because it strips out all the natural variations in colour, kills all the natural highlights, and even though toners can soften the colour, the finished result still looks flat and lifeless. He also believes that you should never have your hair tinted darker than your natural shade – it looks too harsh against your skin-tone – but, if possible, have it tinted three shades lighter. 'And since in a natural head of hair there are at least two or three different shades,' Daniel believes, 'I always use at least three different colours on a client's hair, because different shades give the hair movement, and make it exciting and alive.'

If you decide you do want to try another hair colour, the best bet when you're starting out on a modelling career is to have your hair streaked. The big advantage is that streaks, or highlights, last about ten months and only need retouching every ten or twelve weeks, whereas if you have it tinted, the roots must be retouched every month to avoid that ugly, give-away line. Again, streaks need to be done by a real expert or you would wind up with striped hair. Daniel works on a quarter of an inch at a time, weaving in and out and taking only about ten hairs for each highlight until he's covered the whole head, so that, regardless of where you part your hair or whether you wear it up or down, the effect will be the same.

If you want to change your hair colour or style drastically but not permanently, then your best bet is a wig. There is a vast selection on the market now, ranging from the cheap, man-made fibre ones right through to the very expensive, hand-made, all-European hair wigs, which cost over two hundred pounds. You can buy real hair wigs for considerably less than that, but they're almost inevitably made from Eurasian hair which is coarser and stiffer than European hair, and since its natural state is completely straight, it won't hold a set for more than a few hours. Like some of the better quality man-made wigs, they're fine for photographic sessions, but look too artificial for everyday wear.

The same is true of hairpieces, but if you do decide to buy a cheap one, then look very carefully at the base. In general, the cheaper pieces have very small, stiff, hard bases which not only need a lot of hairgrips to fix them to your own hair, but can also rub against your scalp while you're wearing them, which can also tear your hair.

A few false ringlets can be very useful, too, but be sure you buy those with only a short, stiffened stem at the top, as they give you more hair to play with, and if your hair is long enough to put up, you should always carry a few plaits of crêpe hair in your model bag. When it's unplaited and fluffed out, it's the ideal base for a bun or for one of those rolled hairstyles, and gives you the thickness you need without you having to back-comb your own hair.

With practice, and with the skills of a first-class hairdresser to back you up, you should be able to work minor miracles with your hair. Above all, remember that if, as a model, you take care of your hair, it could well take care of you.

5 Skin

If it's true that beauty is only skin deep, then obviously every model wants to make sure that her skin is as beautiful as it possibly can be. But it's funny stuff, skin. Most of us think of it merely as a sort of wrapper for our bodies – as Allan Sherman says in his parody *You've Gotta Have Skin*, 'it's what keeps your insides in' – but it's much more than that. Unlike your hair, which is simply a protective covering for your head, your skin has a lot of important functions to fulfil – for one thing, the fact that it's more or less waterproof means that it stops water being absorbed or lost in any great quantity and so keeps the amount of fluid your body needs constant. For another, it plays a vital part in regulating your body temperature – when you get too hot, the sweat glands just under the surface of your skin produce moisture to cool you down again – and it's also the means by which your body gets rid of about a fifth of its waste products. It's those, incidentally, along with perspiration, which are the breeding ground for the bacteria which gives off an unpleasant odour if they're allowed to stay on your skin for more than twenty-four hours – which is why a daily bath, or all-over wash is essential.

Your skin is made up of two principal layers – the dermis, which contains all the blood vessels and nerves, and the epidermis, the outer protective layer, which consists of a deep layer of growing cells and a covering – the part of your skin that you actually see – of dead cells which are constantly being shed and replaced by new ones from the layer underneath. So when you cleanse your face, you're not only removing the dirt and the grease, you're also removing dead cells which would otherwise stay on the surface of your skin and give it a rather dull, dingy look.

Although we've got skin everywhere, the area that concerns us most, and the area people are talking about when they say you've got a lovely skin, is your face – with your hands a close second. These are the areas that need most attention, partly because they're on display more than any other area, partly because they're more exposed to the elements, to rapid changes in temperature, to water, and to all the impurities in the atmosphere, and partly because the skin is thinner there than on any other part of your body.

Basically, there are four skin types, determined largely by the activity of the sebaceous glands – the glands in the dermis which produce grease to lubricate your skin. If you have a dry skin – and you have if your face feels tight and papery after you've washed it – then your sebaceous glands are under-active and aren't producing the amount of grease you need. The advantages are that your skin will take make-up well – no excess grease to stop it setting – and isn't susceptible to spots, but the drawbacks are that it doesn't age well since it has little elasticity and will wrinkle easily.

If you have a greasy skin – and you have if your face is naturally rather shiny and the pores around your nose and chin are open and enlarged – then your sebaceous glands are over-active. The advantages are that your skin ages and tans much better than a dry skin, but the price you have to pay is difficulty in getting make-up to stay on – the 'shiny nose' syndrome – and a proneness to spots, blackheads and open pores.

If you've got a normal skin – and you have if you've got no dry, flaky patches and no oily ones either – then your sebaceous glands are producing exactly the right amount of oil, and you're very lucky! There are no draw-backs to this type of skin and the only danger is that, since your skin presents no problems, you might get complacent and neglect it.

The last type is a combination skin – and if you've got a greasy T-shaped area, your forehead, nose and chin, or simply a greasy panel down the centre of your face, but dry cheeks, then that's what you've got. You share the advantages, and disadvantages, of both dry and greasy skins, with the added complication of having to treat the two areas of your face differently.

Although as a general rule skin gets dryer as it gets older, there is nothing you can do to alter your skin type, so you need to recognize early on which type yours is, and treat it accordingly. But whatever your skin type, you'll go a long way towards making the best of it if you learn to cleanse your face properly.

If you've got a normal or oily skin, you can get your face clean with plain, old-fashioned soap and water, since soap will dissolve grease on which all make-up is based, but because you need to use a lot of soap to do so, it's easier to use a cleanser specially formulated to dissolve grease quickly. You can use it by itself, but if you're one of those people who don't feel clean unless you've washed your face, then use a cleanser first and then soap and water. Alternatively, some beauticians recommend cleansing at night, and washing in the morning. Always use a pure unscented soap, such as Simple Soap, on your face, and lukewarm water. Don't use very hot water to open up your pores and get the dirt out, followed by very cold water to close them again – you can achieve the same effect by other, much gentler methods, without running the risk of broken capillaries, those tiny, thread-like red veins you often see on weatherbeaten faces.

Always treat your face gently – don't scrub it, as your mother probably did when you were a child – and for preference use your fingertips rather than a flannel, which unless it's boiled frequently can harbour germs.

If you have a dry skin, though, you should avoid soap and water altogether, since the soap will dissolve even the small amount of grease that your glands are producing, and you can't afford to lose it. You should use a cleansing cream, but before you buy, make sure that it liquefies easily – turns to a light oil on your skin when you rub it on.

If you have a greasy skin, then go for a cleansing milk, which should be as thin as possible – there's already too much grease on your skin and you don't want to make it worse by adding more. For a normal or combination skin, a cleansing milk is the best bet too – if your skin's normal, then you have the right amount of grease anyway, and if you have a combination skin, you don't want to make the greasy parts worse by using a rich dry-skin cleanser on them, and cleansing milk won't do the dry parts any harm.

Whatever your skin-type though, you shouldn't use baby products on your face. They're formulated to soothe baby's bottoms, and they're too rich and greasy for most adult skins. If money is a problem, then you're better off buying a cheap cleanser from a chain-store than baby lotion.

Although it's important to cleanse your face in the morning to get rid of the impurities your skin has expelled during the night, it's absolutely vital to make sure that you've removed every scrap of dirt, grease and make-up from your face before you go to bed. A thorough nightly cleansing routine should be as automatic as cleaning your teeth – something you *always* do, no matter how late you get in or how tired you feel.

Always start by removing your eye make-up, and use either a pad of cotton wool moistened with eye make-up removing oil, or those already impregnated pads you can buy. Don't use ordinary cleanser, because it's too rich for the delicate skin around your eyes and can cause it to become puffy.

Start with your eyebrows and work along them with small semi-circular movements of the pad, from your nose outwards, then back again. Then close your eye, and wipe gently down over your eyelid, right to the tips of your top lashes, then, pushing them gently upwards, wipe on the under-side to remove all traces of mascara. Next, open your eye and, looking upwards, bring the pad down over your lower lashes, then along under-neath them to remove any mascara that may have got on to your skin. Turn the pad over, and use the clean side for your other eye.

To cleanse your face and throat, take a pad of cotton wool about four inches square, apply a little cleansing cream or milk – it's more economical if you damp the cotton wool slightly first to prevent it soaking up too much of the cream or milk – then wrap it round the middle two fingers of your right hand, or left if you happen to be left-handed, gripping it firmly with your index and little fingers. Keeping the middle fingers straight, and starting with your chin, make three circles with the pad around the area, three more round your mouth, three rows of three across each cheek and as many circles as you need to cover your forehead. The circular movement is ideal for two reasons, first, that it doesn't stretch the skin in any one direction, and second, that it's very thorough, making sure that every inch of skin is covered.

After the first cleansing, which is merely to remove the superficial layer of dirt and make-up, turn the cotton wool over, and with the clean side repeat the operation. This second cleansing is probably more important than the first, since it encourages the pores to open and release any grime trapped inside them. If you want to be particularly thorough, then split the cotton wool pad through the middle, and put the two dirty surfaces together so that you have two fresh surfaces to cleanse your face a third and fourth time.

The next step is toning. Toners come in two strengths – the milder ones for dry and normal skins, usually called skin-fresheners, and the stronger ones, astringents, for greasy skins. They are spirit-based, which is why they feel cool and refreshing and make your skin tingle slightly when you apply them. Their function is to close the pores after you've opened them with your cleanser, and by encouraging the blood to run faster through your veins, to improve the general health of your skin. Some products, such as Clinique's Clarifying Lotions, actually help the exfoliating process – the way your skin sheds its dead cells – leaving your skin clearer and more translucent.

Once you've cleansed and toned your skin, the final stage is moisturizing. Moisturizers are a blend of grease and water which work in two ways – first, the grease traps the water against the surface of your skin, which plumps up the cells to make your skin feel soft, while the grease itself counteracts any tendency to dry flakiness and so makes it feel smooth. It can help protect your skin from the effects of the cold or wind, for instance, but as a leading Harley Street skin specialist points out, its effects are only temporary, not cumulative. 'You cannot alter the structure of your skin by putting moisturizers or anything else on it. You can't stop yourself from wrinkling later on, for example, because that depends on what's happening in the deeper layers of your skin, not on the surface, and that's all you're treating when you apply creams. While the preparation is actually on your skin, it does make it look and feel nicer, but if you stop using a moisturizer after a couple of years, your skin will be in no better condition than it would have been if you hadn't put anything on it.'

So if you want to keep your skin looking really good, you can't afford ever to freewheel and neglect it. A daily routine of cleansing, toning and moisturizing is a very good basis from which to work, but if you find it isn't enough, then a weekly face-pack, which really opens up your pores and draws out any stubborn impurities, may make a big difference. There are different kinds for different skins – egg and honey, or lanolin, are good for dry skins, lemon for greasy skins, and though yeast packs are old fashioned they can still do a lot for a problem skin.

So far, we've dealt with trouble-free skins, but almost everyone has to cope with spots at some time in their life. They are a problem for any girl, but for a model they can be catastrophic. The occasional spot is almost in-evitable, and though it's a nuisance it can be coped with quite easily. What isn't so easy to cope with is acne – the outbreak of spots which arrives with the onset of puberty and can last well into your twenties or even longer if you're very unlucky. You can get acne on your face or on your back and chest, or both, though dermatologists aren't certain why it attacks those areas and no others.

The most important factor in determining whether or not you'll get spots, so the skin specialist says, is the way your sebaceous glands react to the hormones in your blood – you don't get spots until your body starts pro-ducing hormones at the onset of puberty, and even girls who are usually spot-free get the occasional blemish just before their period starts, the time when their hormones are hyper-active. 'What happens is that the hormones encourage the cells at the exit of your grease glands to grow and therefore to block the exit. At the same time, they encourage the gland to produce more grease than usual, but as it has no means of escape, the gland enlarges, ruptures into your skin, and since the grease is an irritant, it causes inflam-mation and you get a painful red spot.'

If your grease glands are blocked on the surface of your skin, then washing or using a face-pack or a keratalitic cream – which breaks up the keratin, the top layer of your skin – might remove the blockage and allow the gland to drain, but if it's blocked right the way down inside, nothing you can do superficially will make any difference.

'For bad cases of acne these days,' the skin specialist says, 'there are anti-biotics which work directly on the grease gland and somehow affect the composition of the grease produced, so that if the gland does get blocked and ruptures, the grease won't cause inflammation and you won't get a spot.'

Some doctors still prescribe hormones – oestrogen, particularly – for

Twiggy and her total rapport with a camera – no wonder she was the best known model in the world while she was still in her teens

Above   Location: the tropics. It may look like a dream holiday but she has probably been hard at it since 5.30 am

Opposite   Any model would enjoy modelling a beautiful outfit like this – but the real professional skill comes in making a flour sack look equally stunning

This is Your (Professional) Life – our own cover girl Judi James's portfolio contains a record of all the photographic work she has done so that a potential employer can see how photogenic she is, a quality that isn't obvious in the flesh even to a trained eye

A model girl's first 'live' show – the graduation parade at the London Academy of Modelling

1. GLENDA ALLAN 5'6" 2. AMANDA-LOUISE 5'6" 3. SUZANNE BASS 5'6" 4. SUE BEAVIS 5'8"
5. LINDY BENSON 5'3" 6. JUDY BUTT 5'5" 7. JEANNIE COLLINGS 5'6½" 8. SUE CONWAY 5'5"
9. GILLIAN DUXBURY 5'7" 10. JUDITH DUDLEY 5'2" 11. EVA-LOUISE 5'6" 12. JENNY FINLAY·5'6"
13. PAULA GRIFFIN 5'3" 14. CHRISTIANE HALSTEAD 5'7" 15. PENNY IRVING 5'2" 16. JULIA 5'6"
17. SUSIE JÜÜL 5'8" 18. JULIETTE KING 5'7" 19. SUZY MANDELL 5'6" 20. SUZANNE MILLER 5'

Headsheets like this one, issued by model agencies, adorn the walls of
fashion editors' and advertisers' offices, and are an ideal way of getting
your face known in the right quarters

01-736 0191/2/3

BARA MOLYNEUX 5'3"

22. MARRIANE MORRIS 5'6"

23. RUTH OLIVER 5'4"

24. JO PETERS 5'3"

IKA RINGWALD 5'5"

26. DAWN RODRIGUES 5'8"

27. CLARE RUSSELL 5'4"

28. BOBBY SPARROW 5'7"

NA 5'7"

30. MONICA THIMME 5'7"

31. TIM BLACKSTONE 6'

32. MIKE COX 6'2"

E FARNHAM 6'

34. CURTIS HALL 6'

35. RICHARD HORNE 6'

36. STAN NASH 5'11½"

AUNDERS 6'

38. RIC SAUNDERS 6'

39. SIMON TURNER 6'

40. DAVID WEST 5'11"

Susie Jūūl

Height 5' 8½
Bust 35/34B   Waist 24   Hips 34
Dress Size 10
Shoes 5½   Gloves 5½
Inseam 34   Outside Leg 44
Hair Light Brown   Eyes Blue

Specialities: FASHION, TEENAGE,
             SWIMMING, GOOD LEGS,
             SKI BOBBING, SHOWS

Grösse 1.74
Oberweite 89/86   Taille 61   Hüfte 86
Konfektion 38
Schuhe 38½   Handschuhe 5½
Schrittinnen 86   Schrittaussen 112
Haare Licht Braun   Augen Blau

01- 736 0191/2/3
52 BRITANNIA ROAD, LONDON S.W.6.

The Parker-Sed Agency
2 Hamburg 11 Börsenbrücke 7
Tel 36 78 44
Telex 2163293

MARLOWE. RING CARDS 01 584 8801. AUGUST 1975

BY COURTESY OF C.I.I.

JOHN ADRIAAN for DAVID at H AGENCE

PETE H RITTER

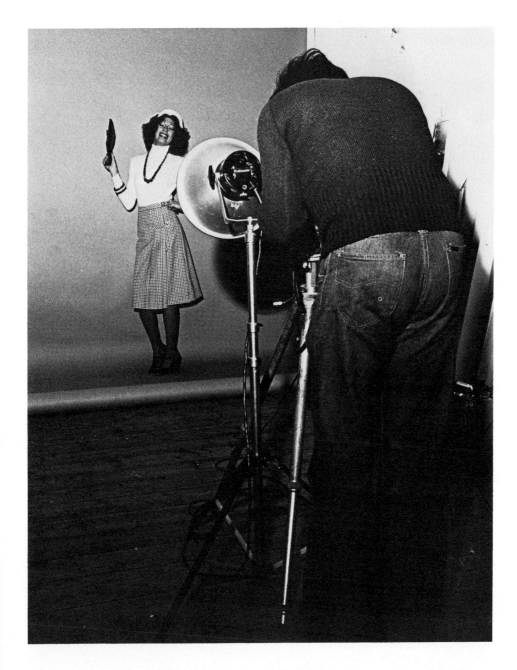

Above Model Amy sparkles in front of Kenneth Bieber's camera as she models a skirt from Gor-Ray's 1976 spring collection

Opposite An index card (both sides are shown), the model girl's calling card, listing her measurements, colouring, sizes and special abilities, and showing as many different aspects of her personality as possible

Above Shirley Anne posing for *Honey* in a draughty underground car-park in November with a wind machine blowing cold air up her legs. A model's life – glamorous?

Opposite Josephine Florent. From shop assistant to *Honey* cover girl in a matter of months, she is one of the few untrained 'discoveries' to make it to the top. (See Chapter 12, 'A day in the life of a photographic model')

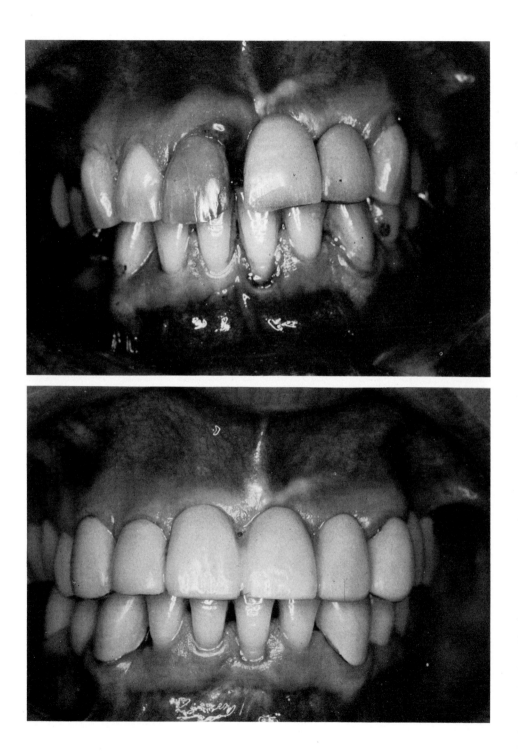

Before and after: the miracles of modern cosmetic dentistry

David Warbeck, with that useful 'prop' cigar, and Philo modelling knitwear for Barrie on a blustery Serpentine

Above   What a difference a smile makes – the two girls in the front really catch the eye. An international swimwear show held in Nice

Opposite above   Singing in the rain. A show for Debenhams, produced by Gregg and Bailey, like most top shows these days was choreographed like a musical

Opposite below   On location. A television commercial for the English Cheese Council being made on location in a railway station

Above Former Hartnell model Yvonne Garfield demonstrates the model girl stance to a class of students at the London Academy of Modelling

Opposite Modelling coats during a 'season' for a buyer at Elgee, a well known wholesale coat house

Above Freddie, a former model who now runs Freddie's, her own model agency, and her partner, Laurie Kuhrt, glance through the portfolio of Nora Hjornevik, a young Scandinavian model, before putting her on their books

Opposite Teenage model Tricia, uncertain whether she's on her head or her heels in this unusual fashion shot

Above   What a lovely pair of legs, pair of legs, pair of legs . . . no, not a centipede, but models practising yoga to keep them in shape physically and to help them cope with the stresses and strains of their careers

Opposite   Making faces – learning to use make-up skilfully is a vital part of any model girl's training and practice makes perfect

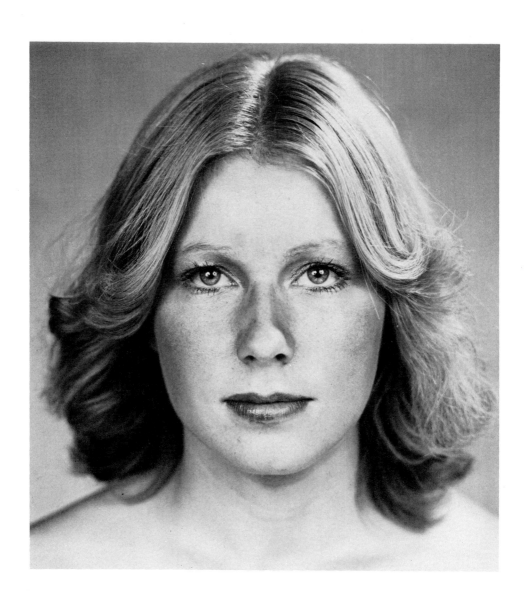

Before and after: these shots show what a difference the right hairstyle and clever make-up can make to any girl

VOGUE

OCT 15
50p

best buys
in fashion
now

what
the country
can do
for you...

beauty,
food,
health,
exercise

splash!
Caribbean
beaches
by Wenda
& Norman
Parkinson

plus!
Men
in
Vogue

Appearing on the cover of *Vogue* is like topping the bill at the London Palladium for any photographic model acute skin problems, but since there may be some undesirable side-effects, many are prescribing antibiotics instead. 'There is a slight problem here too – they *are* antibiotics and if you take them too often you can build up an immunity to them, but taken in small doses and under careful medical super-vision, it's a very safe, effective treatment.'

If you do suffer badly from spots, then it's well worth getting medical advice. You may find that your doctor isn't very sympathetic, on the grounds that he has many genuinely ill people to look after, but if you tell him that you're really worried about the state of your skin, and that it's making you unhappy, then you should get help.

If you only suffer from the occasional spot, then some of the creams and lotions you can buy from the chemist's can help. 'These are basically keratali-tics or "peelers",' says the skin specialist, 'and if you apply them to a spot that's not yet broken, they will take the top off it and help it to dry out more quickly, and because they take off the top layer of skin, they also prevent the glands getting blocked on the surface and so help prevent more spots forming.'

You should never squeeze spots as you'll probably spread the infection in your skin, making the spot bigger so that the eventual scarring will be worse. You can squeeze blackheads – plugs of grease and dirt that get trapped in your pores – but if you do, then be as gentle as you can, use a piece of clean cotton wool, and make sure that your fingers are scrupulously clean too, or else you may infect what was an ordinary blackhead and turn it into a spot.

Even though your metabolism is basically responsible for the spots you may get and there isn't anything you can do to alter it, you can at least make sure that you don't encourage more spots or make those you've already got worse, by cleaning your face two or three times a day and by eating sensibly.

At one time, everyone who suffered from spots was told not to eat greasy, fatty foods or rich, sweet things like cream cakes or chocolate, but medical opinion these days tends towards the view that where diet is concerned it's impossible to generalize. 'Some patients find that fried food and chocolate do make their spots worse,' the skin specialist says, 'but on the other hand I have patients who live on lettuce leaves and who are covered in spots too! You must simply use your common sense – if you find a particular food makes your spots worse, then cut it out.' Some girls find that Vitamin C helps improve the condition of their skins – plenty of fresh fruit, citrus fruit, especially, and vegetables – while others find yeast tablets, rich in Vitamin B, help clear up their spots.

Sunshine can help a spotty skin too – the sun acts as a 'peeler' and helps unblock blocked glands – but in excess it doesn't do any type of skin much good. Strong sunshine, such as you'd find in the Mediterranean and tropical countries, can not only burn your skin, it can also destroy the elasticity, so that you will wrinkle very badly in middle age or even earlier. Look at Australian girls – many of them have very tough leathery skins before they've reached thirty, as a result of too much exposure to the sun. So, tempting though it is to stretch out on the beach and get a glorious tan, if you want your skin to look good when you're thirty-five – don't.

Obviously your face is the most important area when it comes to skin care, but don't forget your hands. They're very important, no matter what kind of modelling you do. Romantic evening dresses and dishpan hands do not go together, and if a photographer asks you to rest your cheek on your hand, even the softest, smoothest skin in the world won't look good against rough, chapped red hands. And, of course, if you have got beautiful hands, you can make a very good living as a hand model, in advertisements not only for hand creams and nail varnish, but for almost everything from jewellery and glassware to washing-up liquid and baked beans.

To keep your hands looking good, you should keep them out of water as much as possible – wear rubber gloves for washing and washing-up, and use a good, rich hand cream, such as Christie's Lanolin, every time you've had to put them in water.

To keep the rest of your body smooth and supple, you can use a bath oil or foam, but if you are in the least susceptible to cystitis, as many women are, then avoid putting anything in your bath water, because the chemicals can make the condition worse or even cause an attack. Your best bet is to use a body lotion all over after you've bathed, to counteract the drying effect of water on your skin, but again, you're better off with a cheap, purpose-made product than with a baby lotion.

Skin, of all your natural assets, is perhaps the most precious to you as a model. If something awful happens to your hair, you can get away with wigs. If you lose a tooth, you can have it replaced with a crown. But if something goes badly wrong with your skin, then even the cleverest make-up won't be able to hide it totally, so it really is worth investing the time and effort in keeping it as near perfection as you can.

6 Make-up

There is hardly a woman alive – including that rarest of creatures, the perfect natural beauty – whose looks can't be, if not improved, then certainly enhanced, by the skilful use of make-up, and for the majority of us, whose looks fall well short of perfection, make-up can straighten out irregularities, hide imperfections, make the most of our good points, and by helping to give us a face we're able to present to the world, be a great morale-booster, too.

If you're modelling though, and your face is your fortune, then real skill with cosmetics is not merely a useful asset, it's absolutely essential. Admittedly, if you're doing beauty shots for *Vogue* or a commercial to launch a whole new range of cosmetics, there'll be a highly skilled make-up artist to do your face for you, but until you get to that stage – indeed, if you *want* to get to that stage – you must be able to do almost as good a job on your face yourself.

It's impossible to stress too highly how important it is to be skilful with make-up, especially if you want to do photographic modelling. You'd be surprised at how many of the top girls you would probably not recognize off duty because, without their make-up on, their faces are undistinguished, almost plain.

When you're modelling, there are three main reasons for wearing make-up: to accentuate your good points, to disguise your bad ones, and to bring your face as close as possible to the classic look, which is an oval shape, with high cheek-bones and well-proportioned, evenly spaced features.

Obviously you'll wear a heavier, more colourful make-up when you're working than you normally would, because, whether you're working in a salon or a showroom or a photographic studio, you'll be working under artificial light which drains colour away, so that with only your everyday make-up on, you'd look washed out and colourless.

It's important, when you're starting out on your career, to get used to wearing a full make-up every day – for one thing you never know when you may be sent off to an audition at a moment's notice, and for another, you need as much practice at making up your face as you can get. Experiment at home in the evenings, too, with different colours and different styles – try making-up only one side of your face at a time so that, by comparing it with the other side, you can see exactly what effect the various products are having – what makes your cheeks look slimmer, for example, what makes your eyes look bigger.

But you can't hope to do a really good job unless you have the right equipment. You need a solid, wide working surface to put all your tools and bottles and tubes on, preferably one that wipes clean easily, and a large mirror that's well-lit both during the day and at night. You'll also find a magnifying mirror essential for close work such as checking that every detail of your eye make-up is right. You'll need a head-band to keep your hair off your face while you're working on it, a large box of tissues, cotton wool, cotton buds – good for blending in eyeshadows so that there are no hard lines – and, most important, an assortment of sable brushes in a variety of different widths and thicknesses, which you'll need for applying almost everything from eyeliner to powdered blusher. Sable is the most expensive but it is also the best, and with care will last you a lifetime.

And then of course, there is your make-up itself. Given that your skin has been properly cleansed, toned and moisturized, the first thing you need is a good foundation and a 'good' foundation is the one that is right for your skin. It could be a liquid, it could be a gel, it could be a cream – it's unlikely to be a powder-creme block, since it doesn't go on to your skin anything like as smoothly and as evenly as you need. It could costy sixty pence, it could cost three pounds, but all that really matters is that it looks good on you. Admittedly, it isn't always easy to find the right foundation straight-away – most of us, models or not, have got an assortment of barely touched tubes and jars that 'looked all right in the shop' – and it's largely a question of shopping around. Most big department stores stock all the major brands, but you can only try the tester out on your wrist or hand, and the skin on your face is rarely precisely the same colour.

If you live in or near London, it's worth making a journey to Joan Price's Face Place in Cadogan Street, SW3, where you can try out most of the major brands on your face before you buy, and if you're prepared to do the rounds of the cosmetic companies' own showrooms, you can try out their own products there. If that's not possible, then your best bet is to decide whether your skin is light, medium or dark, then go for a neutral, beigey shade in that range. Avoid anything that has a pinkish tinge as it's likely to turn orange on your skin after an hour or so.

If you're black, then the problem is much more acute. Until Outdoor Girl introduced their Tawny range a couple of years ago, there was no foundation made specially for darker skins and all that was available was theatrical pancake, which was fine for photographic work, but too thick and too greasy for everyday wear. Tawny products are widely available now, and some of the other manufacturers have introduced some darker shades into their normal range of foundations, but if you still can't find one that's right for your skin, then you'll have to try shops in immigrant areas which import cosmetics from America, though of course they will be much more expensive.

You'll also need a blusher, and when you're learning, you'll probably find a cream one, either in a jar or in stick form, easier to handle than powder, because you can control more easily exactly where the colour goes. Again, avoid anything that is too pink – warm colours, browns, corals, plums, are much more flattering. If you are black, then choose a darker colour – coffee or maroon, for instance – that blends with your skin tone. Blushers don't present the same problem as foundations and most ordinary cosmetic firms from Mary Quant to Estée Lauder produce shades that are perfect for black skins.

You'll need a highlighter, usually creamy white or a pale golden brown if you have a black skin, and a shader, which will probably be brown.

You can't have too many eyeshadows in almost every conceivable shade, though the powdered and cream ones are much better for modelling than the greasier kind that usually come in little pots because they stay on much longer, and don't streak in the creases of your eyes. You should also have an eyeliner and matching mascara – in a basic colour like black or brown and perhaps in something a little different too, like navy or plum, depending on your colouring.

You should have a variety of lipsticks, too, in good strong colours, including at least one bright, warm red. Throw out any pale, pearly pinks you may have left in your make-up bag – not only are they very unfashionable now, they don't show up in 'live' fashion shows, and come out white in photographs. You'll also need a clear lip gloss which you'll wear over every lipstick or, if you're not wearing any, on its own.

You should always try to match your nail varnish to your lipstick, but in any case always go for a good, strong colour – red, plum, brown – though it's best to avoid the more unusual blues, blacks and greens when you're working. Make sure that your nail varnish is never chipped or cracked, and that your nails are manicured into a neat, oval shape. Long talons are not only rather unattractive, they're also impractical – they're much more likely to break, for instance, during rapid changes of outfit in a fashion show, and may even snag the clothes you're pulling on. If you do break a nail and you haven't got a false one that you can stick on, then file the remaining nails down to a similar length – nothing looks worse than an assortment of long and short nails on the same hand.

When you're starting out on your career and getting yourself equipped, there are so many different products on the market that it's almost impossible to know what to buy. Unfortunately there aren't any worthwhile short cuts, and it's very much a question of trial and error, of finding out what suits you, whether it's the cheapest of its kind or the most expensive.

Barbara Daly, who is probably the top photographic make-up artist in the country right now – she did Princess Anne's make-up for her wedding, and for the pre-wedding photographs – believes that price isn't a very reliable guide to just how good a product is. 'In my make-up box, I've got everything from a tenpenny Rimmel Hide'n'Heal stick to Estée Lauder foundations at over three pounds a go! I've got a lot of the Boots' Number 17 range, for instance, because I think it's excellent, and that's one of the cheapest on the market. But I do think it's worth paying the extra for things like eyeshadow – the colours and textures of the expensive ones are so much better than cheaper kinds. There's just no comparison between a Biba eye gloss, say, and a Revlon Ultima 11 shadow.'

The same is true, she believes, of lipsticks – it's the colour you pay for, and the more expensive the lipstick, the more subtle, the more unusual, the colours are likely to be. 'When you're modelling, I think your attitude to buying make-up is different. If you're just an ordinary girl, you might think "That eighty-pence lipstick is almost as nice as the three pound one, so I'll settle for that." But if you're modelling and the three pound is right, then you should buy it. It's an investment in your career.'

Your make-up will vary, naturally, with the type of work you're doing. For a live fashion show, for instance, it will be as classic and as simple as possible so as not to detract from the clothes you're modelling.

Start with your foundation, and whether you apply it with your finger-tips or with a damp sponge, use *as little as possible*. 'The mistake most girls make,' Barbara Daly believes, 'is to use too much and to swamp their skin. If your skin is good, then you're only using foundation to give it colour and to even out the skin tone, so you want to let as much of it show through as you can.'

Once your foundation is on – and do remember always to make sure that it doesn't stop suddenly at your jawline in a tidemark – apply your high-lighter, blusher and shader. In general terms, a highlighter reflects light and so makes the area to which you apply it more prominent – the tops of your cheek-bones, for instance – and a shader absorbs light, and so pushes the area into the background. Used under your cheek-bones it will create interesting hollows if there are none, or exaggerate those already there; used down the sides of your nose, it will make it seem slimmer, and it can also help soften a heavy jaw or shorten a long chin. Blusher works in a mysterious way for it not only adds colour to your cheeks, it seems to make your eyes sparkle and your whole skin glow. You should use it with care though, since red is the colour to which the eye always goes first. As a general rule, keep it away from the centre of your face – like your highlighter and shader, it should only be applied to the area between your hairline and an imaginary line drawn down your face from the outer corners of your eyes. If you've got a very dark skin, then shaders won't show up, so you'll have to shape your face with a highlighter – not too pale – and blusher used in the hollows you find when you suck in your cheeks.

Once you've finished shaping and shading your face, and before you apply your eye make-up, you should set your make-up with powder, and a fine, translucent, colourless one like Leichner's Blending Powder is ideal. If you apply it properly, by *rolling* it on to your skin with a piece of cotton wool, then it's completely invisible, but it is essential for keeping your make-up on under hot lights and hectic conditions. Powder your eyelids, too, to ensure that you have a good, matt surface for your eyeshadow.

Fashions in make-up change almost as fast as fashions in clothes, and nowhere is it more obvious than around the eyes. In the late sixties, it was thick black liner and spidery false lashes on the top lid only; in the early seventies, it was delicate shadows all round the eye, no eyeliners and mascara only, top and bottom. But regardless of the changes, there are certain rules that always apply, for example, toning your eye make-up with your clothes. It can be a problem if you're modelling twenty different outfits in a show, and you might think that a neutral colour such as grey or brown would be the answer, but it isn't, since they tend not to show up under bright lights. It's best to stick to fairly bright colours – blues, greens, mauves – in a tone that goes with the majority of your outfits. If you're black, then your eyes are probably your most outstanding feature anyway, and you need to do very little to draw attention to them. You *can* wear very bright colours, though, in striking and unusual combinations, in a way that most white girls can't, but you still need to be a little careful or you could wind up looking like a panda. 'Nothing gives away a girl's lack of expertise with make-up faster than thick, gooey eyeshadow, badly applied,' says Gerda Webster, Jamaican-born model and make-up consultant, 'so until you've had lots of practice, and know what you're doing, avoid the bright colours and stick to the darker, smoky shades instead!' Avoid frosted eyeshadows, since they tend to come out white, and to make your eyes look puffy.

It's unlikely these days that you'll be asked to wear false eyelashes, unless you're doing a 'live' show in an enormous room, but you should know how to put them on and make them look as natural as possible, and always carry them with you in your make-up kit, just in case.

For fashion shows, your eyebrows should be well-groomed and glossy, but for photographic sessions it's absolutely essential that they're in first-class shape. If they're dark, they'll show up very strongly, and even the smallest imperfection will be all too clear. You should keep them plucked in a neat arch, but don't make them twenties-thin. As a rough guide to the ideal shape, hold a pencil against the side of your nose – where it meets your brow line, the eyebrow should begin. Then swing the pencil through forty-five degrees, and stop – that's where the brow should finish. If you find plucking your eyebrows painful, try rubbing the area with an ice cube first – it not only deadens the skin, but makes the hair follicle contract so that the hair is easier to grip with the tweezers.

If you're blonde but have dark eyebrows, it's worth having them bleached, only do go to a professional and don't try to do it yourself. If your eyelashes are fair, then think about having them dyed, because it would save you having to use so much mascara.

Again, in photographs your eyelashes show up in minute detail, so they must be immaculate too – each eyelash must be separate and not stuck to its neighbour with mascara. Whether you use the roll-on wand kind, or a solid block and brush, it's better to apply two or three thin coats than one thick one, and use a dry, clean brush to separate your lashes between each coat. Some models actually go to the trouble of separating their lashes with a pin when they've applied the final coat, but if you're careful as you put it on, that shouldn't be necessary. If it's a black and white shot, the colour of your eye make-up won't matter, but if it's a colour shot, then choose a shade that tones with what you're wearing, the colour that's closest to your face especially.

You'll still wear foundation, highlighter, shader and blusher, of course, but they'll need to be applied much more subtly than they would be for a live fashion show, since you're much closer to the camera than you would be to an audience. Barbara Daly uses the same amount of make-up on a model's face for a photograph as she would for a live show, but she blends it in much more carefully, so that there are no hard lines and it's impossible to tell where one colour ends and another begins. It takes her about forty minutes to do a girl's face, and most of that time is spent in blending the colours into each other. Barbara Daly uses brushes and her fingers – brushes to apply colour accurately, and fingers to blend and soften the lines.

Your lips must always be soft and glossy – if yours tend to be dry, try wearing Innoxa's Lip Barrier Cream, either by itself when you're not wearing any make-up, or under lipstick, which incidentally it will help to stay on longer. You should outline your lips with a soft crayon, making any adjustments to size or shape, then apply lipstick with a brush, because, again, you can be more accurate. You should always wear a gloss on top of your lipstick, whether it's fashionable or not, and if you don't need lipstick for a black and white shot, say, then wear gloss by itself.

If you're unlucky enough to have a spot on the day you've been booked for a photographic session, then tell the photographer, no matter how well you can camouflage it with make-up, because he can arrange the lighting in such a way that there is no chance of it showing up on the finished photograph.

For television commercials, the most important points to remember are that the camera will make you look about a stone heavier in weight than you actually are, and that it will accentuate any small fault in your face, so you need to be especially skilful with shaders and highlighters to make your face look as small as possible, and your features as even as you can. If your nose is too long, then you can shorten it with a little shader on the tip, if it's crooked, then a line of highlighter down the centre of the bone will help to straighten it out.

Obviously, make-up can only do so much to disguise a facial fault, so in the case of protruding ears or a nose that's too big or misshapen as the result of a childhood accident, say, it might be worth considering plastic surgery. Apart from the fact that you have to have it done privately and it is extremely expensive (a rhinoplasty – 'nose job' to the uninitiated – costs from about three hundred pounds) it is a major step and you should only contemplate taking it if you *genuinely* believe that your nose or your ears are what's holding you back from a successful modelling career, and if other unbiased people, your agent for instance, believe it too. As a well-known Harley Street plastic surgeon points out, you won't get an honest, dispassionate opinion from your family or boyfriend. 'Your parents have known you all your life and love you the way you are, and since they created you, nose and all, they'll feel that your wish to alter it is somehow a criticism of them.' Once you've made up your mind that you really do want plastic surgery, then you'll have to convince your family doctor of that fact before he'll refer you to a plastic surgeon. If you know of a good one whom you'd like to see, then ask your doctor to send you to him, as you cannot approach the surgeon direct. You must be realistic: don't go along with a photograph of Audrey Hepburn and ask for a nose like hers. No reputable plastic surgeon works like that – he has to take into account the rest of your features, the shape and size of your face, if he wants to produce a natural result. 'Ten or fifteen years ago,' says the plastic surgeon, 'plastic surgery did often rob the face of all its individuality – in America for instance, the short "bobbed" nose was fashionable because it was young-looking and photographed well, but it was often done without proper regard for the patient's features with the result that it looked very unnatural.'

Be prepared for the fact that you'll almost certainly come round from the operation to find yourself with two beautiful black eyes, and that it will take weeks for your nose to settle finally into its new shape.

Some people still consider plastic surgery almost immoral – spending all that money out of sheer vanity! – but if you really want to be a successful model, then the money you spend on your looks, whether it's a three-pound foundation or a three-hundred-pound 'nose job', is *not* vanity – it's an investment in your career.

7   Tools of the trade

As a model, your working life revolves around clothes, but of course they are almost always other people's, chosen for you by somebody else and often 'accessorized' for you by somebody else too, so from that point of view your own dress sense or lack of it may not seem terribly important. In almost every other way, though, it is crucial.

When you walk into a fashion editor's office or a photographer's studio, you will inevitably be judged to some extent on first impressions, and from your own choice of outfit a perceptive prospective employer can tell at once whether you have that feeling for clothes, for fabrics and colours, that a really good model has. If you arrive in a pair of white slingback shoes, with dark textured stockings, a Crimplene mini-dress and chunky knit, clashing cardigan, you're hardly likely to inspire your would-be employer with the confidence that you'll work wonders for the outfit or the product he wants you to sell.

Style is to a large extent instinctive – something you're born with, not something you can acquire from reading books, though it is possible to learn a few basic rules that will help you avoid the worst excesses. For example, always tone colours, and never mix textures and styles – a thick tweedy cardigan just does not go over a chiffon evening dress.

It's made even more complicated by the fact that good dress sense is to a large extent to do with taste, which is very personal and individual. Among your mother's circle, a rhinestone imitation of one of the Queen's brooches on the lapel of a suit may be thought of as the height of good taste, whereas none of your friends would be seen dead dressed in that way. And, of course, it's very much to do with fashion. Five years ago, a skirt three inches below the knee looked dowdy on any woman, no matter what her age. Now a skirt three inches above the knee looks very dated, even faintly tarty.

If you don't know instinctively what is right for now – and very few girls do when they are just starting to organize their wardrobe – then look at the fashion magazines and what the *trends* are. Don't follow high fashion too

slavishly – for one thing, it changes so fast that it can prove a very expensive
pastime, and for another you need to be supremely self-confident and to
get it right down to the last detail if you are going to carry it off successfully.

Remember that dress sense doesn't depend on how much money you
have to spend – you only need look at pictures of the world's richest women
in the papers or see how many of them feature regularly on the list of the
World's Worst Dressed Women to realize that. Of course, it is less effort to
look good if you have unlimited funds. You don't have to spend every lunch
hour for two weeks looking for a sweater that looks like a Missoni – you can
simply walk into Brown's and pay forty pounds for the real thing. But if
you are prepared to spend the time and you have the flair, you can look just
as good on a budget.

First of all, you must decide what style and which colours suit you best.
Obviously when you're modelling you must be able to adapt so that you
look good in almost anything, but privately, if you look best in casual
clothes, trousers and shirts, then stick to them and avoid neat little tailored
dresses, or a really freaky thirties look. If brown suits you, then plan your
wardrobe around that colour – go for creams, beiges, camels, rusts, oranges,
yellows, as well as brown itself, and you'll find you not only have plenty of
variety, but a wardrobe that is colour co-ordinated as well. And that, perhaps
above anything else, is the key to good dress sense on a tight budget. Since
money is limited, you must make sure that every single item you buy really
earns its keep – every shirt and sweater must go with several skirts or pairs of
trousers – so impulse buys are out. That bright red sweater may be a nice
cheerful colour but surely the camel shade, which will go with your black
suit, your dark brown trousers, your rust overdress, as well as your jeans, is a
more sensible buy?

When you go out shopping for clothes, decide what you want before you
go and don't be sidetracked. It's very easy at the end of a long day, when
you've failed to find what you're looking for, or when the shop assistant is
being particularly persistent, to give in and settle for anything, but in ninety-
nine cases out of a hundred, you'll regret it. Almost everyone has a couple of
impulse buys hanging unworn in the wardrobe, but when you're modelling,
your clothes are part of the tools of your trade, and you cannot afford to
make mistakes.

The golden rule is 'always think hard, before you buy'. That fur-trimmed
winter coat may be beautiful but wouldn't it be wiser to spend the money
on a classic trench-coat style mac that will look equally good over skirts,
dresses, smart trousers and jeans, that can look smart or casual depending on
how you wear it, that will be as useful in winter with a couple of sweaters

under it as it is in summer when you only need something light, and that will never date?

With other garments, you must decide whether it is worth spending the money and buying yourself the best. Where trousers are concerned, for instance, it is worth it. A superbly cut pair in a good quality fabric, and in a colour such as black, will always look good both for daytime and evening wear, no matter what fashion is saying about trousers, and in the long run will give you much better value than several cheap pairs in the latest style which will probably 'seat' or crease very unattractively at the crotch, or go shiny after a few wearings, and which of course will almost certainly date.

But with sweaters, plain ones especially, what you pay for is the colour – the more expensive the garment, the more subtle the colours are likely to be – so provided you avoid the so-called fashion colours, and stick to neutrals, such as black, white, grey or beige, you'll find Marks and Spencer's polo-necked wool sweaters just as good as other makes twice the price.

The chain-stores are also good places to buy tights and underwear, especially now that they are making bikini briefs in cotton, which are better than nylon on two counts. First, they're better from a health point of view since cotton is both absorbent and porous – gynaecologists believe that nylon briefs are in part responsible for the increase in diseases such as thrush and cystitis since they don't allow the air to get to your body – and second, they're better practically speaking too, because you can boil cotton to keep it white, whereas you can't boil nylon, and nothing looks worse than white nylon underwear that has gone grey or yellow.

You should always wear matching bra and briefs, and if they are supposed to be white, then make sure they are. If you're a freelance show model or a photographic model, you'll be spending a lot of time in changing rooms in your bra and briefs, and nothing is more off-putting for your colleagues and employers than grubby underwear. Avoid blatantly sexy underwear too, both the 'black-lace-red-nylon' variety and the stretchy kind with so-called saucy jokes printed on them – they'll make you seem rather immature and may give people the wrong idea about you.

Again, from a health point of view, it's better to wear your briefs under your tights, since tights worn next to the skin have the same disadvantage as nylon briefs, but if you prefer to wear them over, then make sure the tights don't show above your briefs.

Tights should tone with your clothes when possible – black with a black skirt, dark brown with brown, navy with navy and so on, but with very strong colours such as pillar-box red or emerald green you'd be safer with black – and always with your shoes. The effect of matching tights and shoes is to make your legs look longer and slimmer and your feet smaller. Never wear shoes that are lighter than your tights – the effect is to focus attention on your feet and make them look enormous.

With shoes the price they are now, you must look after them. Keep them polished, put shoe-trees or tightly packed crumpled newspaper in them when you're not wearing them and take them to the menders before the heels have worn right down. Your working shoes, especially if you're a free-lance show model, take such a lot of punishment – not only your own feet slipping in and out of them four or five times a day, but other people's treading on them in a cluttered dressing-room – that you'll be lucky if they're still wearable at the end of a season.

Take care of your clothes too – that way they will not only look better but they will last you that much longer, too. Remember that a stitch in time literally does save nine – if you sew up that hem when you first see a few stitches coming undone, you won't catch your heel in it and rip the whole lot down just when you least want that to happen. Same with buttons. Sew them on the moment they begin to feel loose – don't wait till they fall off and you lose them. Of course, you can always find another button that will match, to the naked eye, anyway, but you'd be surprised how different from the other buttons it may look in a photograph, when it's too late to do anything about it.

Try and get into the habit of checking your clothes every night as you take them off, and *never* put anything back into your wardrobe that needs cleaning, washing or repairing. There is nothing more irritating than dashing to the wardrobe to get out the white shirt a client has especially asked you to take along to a session, only to find that the collar and cuffs are grubby.

Always air your clothes when you take them off – hanging them in a draught is ideal, since the air helps clear the smells of the day, cigarette smoke, traffic fumes, cooking, and so on, and also helps the creases to drop out – and don't put them away in the wardrobe till the next day.

Do be careful how you wash your clothes – just to throw everything into your launderette bag and hope for the best is asking for trouble. White nylon underwear will keep its colour much longer if you wash it by hand in lukewarm water with the mildest detergent you can find. If it does go grey or yellow, then you can either try one of the nylon whiteners there are on the market or you could dye it with cold tea, which will turn it a rather attractive pale flesh colour.

Even if the label inside your sweater says you can wash it in a machine, you're safer washing it by hand, squeezing it gently to get rid of excess moisture, then drying it flat on a towel. If it's a really good quality, expensive sweater, it's probably best to have it dry-cleaned, just in case.

If you are building up a wardrobe on a slender budget, then you'll find that accessories can be extremely valuable in giving you that chic, expensively dressed look, and it is worth investing in good ones. If you've got eight or ten pounds to spend, it's very tempting when you're starting out to rush off and buy a couple of cheap skirts or a skirt and sweater with it, but if you spent it instead on a really good leather belt or a silk scarf by Hermès or St Laurent, you'd find that they make the chain-store shirt and trousers you already have look four times as expensive as they were.

When you're doing fashion shots for a magazine, or for an advertisement, you'll probably find that all your accessories, from shoes and handbags right down to scarves and jewellery are provided for you – indeed, some magazines, such as *Vogue*, have special fashion editors who do nothing but 'accessorize' photographic sessions – but in other cases, you'll be expected to provide your own. To carry them around you'll need a model bag, either a tote bag – one of those large canvas shoppers which the chain-stores sell, for instance – or a large sausage-shaped one. When you're just starting out and haven't got much money to spend, it's tempting to make do with a suitcase, but don't – nothing looks more unprofessional.

A few years ago, a model girl's bag was almost a joke – it contained everything but the kitchen sink and it was said you could always tell a model by the over-developed muscles in her right arm from carrying it round London day after day. These days, a surprising number of girls don't bother to equip themselves properly – much to the annoyance of fashion editors and stylists, who find themselves having to dash off to the shops half-way through a session because the model hasn't brought the right scarf or the red knee-socks she was asked to bring. Until you're right at the top of the tree and are such a good model that you'll still get work no matter how much you irritate photographers and fashion editors by your inefficiency, you should be like a Boy Scout and always – *always* – be prepared.

You'll need two or three pairs of shoes – the ubiquitous black patent court shoes, a pair of plain lighter-coloured shoes, and a sportier pair for trousers. Your agent will probably tell you in advance what kind of a session it is likely to be so you can judge accordingly what you will need – no point in taking your boots along if it's bikinis or evening wear! You'll also want three or four pairs of tights in different colours; knee-socks; a thin, packable wrap – a kimono is ideal – to slip on between outfits; two or three sets of underwear in different colours and styles; black leather gloves, white cotton ones, and possibly a long evening pair; a variety of scarves, plain and patterned, silk, chiffon and cotton, long and square – compared to French and Italian women, we British are notoriously ham-fisted when it comes to tying scarves, but as a model you must know how to tie a scarf properly, either round your neck to dress up a plain shirt or dress or fill in the neckline of a coat, or round your head if it's a windy day or your hair isn't at its best. You should also have several belts in different colours and widths; some good costume-jewellery – gilt chains, the best you can afford, since the very cheap ones do look very cheap, and a string of imitation pearls, again the best you can afford, because they go with most things and are very flattering to almost every type of skin. The same is true of plain pearl stud earrings and if you have nothing else you should have a pair of those. Gilt, 'jet' or 'tortoiseshell' studs, and perhaps a pair of gilt gipsy hoops would be very useful too.

You'll endear yourself to your employers if you also have the odd pair of sunglasses, a selection of hair slides, combs and ribbons – a length of thin black velvet ribbon, for instance, can be very useful not only for tying back your hair but for wearing round your neck, either by itself or with a brooch to dress up a plain evening dress. A small pair of scissors, a needle and cotton, black and white, and a selection of safety pins are invaluable. You'll also need your hairpiece, or wig if you have one, your heated hair rollers, and an adaptor, in case the plug doesn't fit the sockets at the studio, and in fact all the equipment you need for doing your hair, plus tissues, cotton wool, deodorant, foot spray, soap, toothpaste and brush, sanitary protection – you simply cannot afford to be caught without it, ever! – your small magnifying mirror, your nail kit, your make-up box, your diary, and an *A to Z* of London.

Never get blasé about your model bag – don't assume that everything is there just because it usually is, or that because you haven't been asked to wear a strapless bra for a couple of years, you no longer need to carry it with you. Check it every night before you go to bed to make sure that everything is clean and in good repair. Don't leave it till the morning, no matter how tired you are, because you may forget or oversleep and have to leave in such a hurry that there isn't time. Remember, your model bag isn't merely a piece of luggage – it is your way of life.

8　Your agent and you

Without doubt, the single most important person in your working life, once you start out on your career as a model, is your agent, and if you find yourself a really good one, then he or she will not only find you work and guide your career, but he'll act as adviser, friend and father – or mother – confessor, too. It's almost impossible to operate successfully as a model – a freelance model especially – without an agent. For one thing, agents are the people clients contact when they're looking for models, and for another, they or their staff are sitting at the end of a telephone for nine hours a day, ready to answer queries and take bookings for you – something you simply haven't the time to do yourself if you're out seeing potential clients or on a job.

Your agent also looks after the financial side of your career. He will get the best possible rates for a job, look after all the paperwork, such as sending out invoices, and though he won't cope with your National Insurance contributions and your Income Tax – for which you're responsible if you're freelance – he will probably be able to recommend a good accountant who knows the specific problems that models have.

Incidentally, never discuss money with a photographer or potential client – always refer them to your agent. For one thing, when you're just starting out, you won't know how much a particular firm or studio can afford to pay, and for another, why expose yourself unnecessarily to the embarrassment that discussing money usually creates, especially if you're arguing about what you're worth?

Finding the right agent is almost as important as finding the right husband, since your professional life will revolve very closely around him, and the best place to start looking is at the top. There are about twenty-five or thirty reputable model agencies in London (the best are listed at the end of this book), but agencies close or amalgamate, new ones open, established ones go through a sticky patch or suddenly blossom all the time. The Westminster City Council can give you a list of the agencies they license, but unfortunately a licence isn't a watertight guarantee of reputability, so your best bet is to ask someone in the business or, failing that, contact the fashion or beauty department of a magazine, which would certainly be able to tell you which agencies they are currently using most often.

Before you start doing the rounds, though, it's worth ringing to check that the agency does take on newcomers, because there are one or two who'll only take on girls with a couple of years' experience behind them, so no matter how much potential you may have, you'd still be wasting your time.

Remember that all reputable agents work exclusively on commission – run a mile from anyone who asks you for an enrolling fee, because not only will you lose that money, but the 'agency' will almost certainly get you no work and do your morale a lot of harm – which means that unless he gets you work, he won't make any money out of you, so before he'll take you on, you'll have to convince him that you are a good commercial proposition. First impressions are important, so always go along for an interview looking your best, and since a large part of modelling is the ability to sell your personality, you must prove to the agent that you can do it by selling your personality to him. Evelyn Thorsen of the London Model Agency is put off by girls who are negative in their approach. 'I don't like girls coming in and saying "My face isn't terribly good and I'm a bit too big round the hips, but . . ." Don't tell people what's wrong with you – they'll find out for themselves soon enough – emphasize your good points!'

Although top agents are very busy people, they are constantly on the look-out for new faces, so most of them will be prepared to see you. 'We try and see every girl we possibly can,' says Tony Askew of Askew's Agency, 'whether she's had experience or training or not. It does help if she brings some photographs with her, just so we can get some idea of what she looks like in front of a camera, because it's impossible to tell just by looking at a girl whether she's photogenic or not. But, in any case, if we think she's got potential, we'd arrange to get some test shots of her done.'

It's not a good idea to spend a lot of money on photographs before you've found yourself an agent – the one who eventually takes you on might think the photographs give you entirely the wrong image, so all that hard-earned money you've spent will be wasted. Beware of any agent who asks you for money to pay for photographs, because a good one will do his utmost to get as many test shots as he can done free or for very little.

Don't be disheartened if three or four agencies turn you down, because agencies *do* specialize – some in fashion shows, others in catalogue and advertising photography, or in high fashion – and maybe you're just not quite right for them. Askew's, for instance, only take on about one girl for every ten they see, but they do try and help by recommending other agencies which might be more suitable.

Of course, it's very flattering when an agent is keen to take you on, but before you agree be sure that you like him and that you trust his judgement. If there are going to be constant conflicts and clashes of personality between you, then your working relationship isn't going to be very productive.

It is possible to be on the books of more than one agency, but it isn't a good idea unless you're doing more than one type of work – say, show modelling and photographic work – and have a different agent for each. If you're only doing one type of work, you could find yourself being sent to the same audition by both agencies, in which case, if you get the job, there will be problems about which one gets the commission on your fee, or being booked for different jobs at the same time, so that you have to let one or other of your agencies down, which won't make you very popular.

Once you've found an agent whom you like and who likes you, he will probably ask you to sign a form. It is *not* a contract – it doesn't mean he is obliged to find you work or that you are obliged to stay with him. All it *does* state is that you agree to pay him an agreed percentage on fees for any work that he gets for you. If he finds you a permanent job, then you'll pay him the equivalent of one week's wages – depending on your age and experience, approximately what a junior shorthand typist in London would be earning. If you're freelance, doing either 'seasons', shows or photographic work, your agent will take his commission of between fifteen and twenty-five per cent of what you earn. Some agencies will pay you in advance of getting the fee from the client – at the end of the month in which you did the job, for instance – and will charge you a higher percentage for doing so. Others will charge you the higher percentage anyway, without providing you with that service, so it is worth checking exactly how much commission you will be paying before you sign on with an agency.

In the case of photographic work and some shows, your agent will invoice the client on your behalf, receive the money and take his commission before he pays you, but if you're doing a season, you'll be paid direct every Friday, so once you've finished your four, or six weeks' work, you'll have to settle up with your agent and pay him.

If a client whom your agent found for you books you again for another show or season or photographic session and the client contacts you direct himself, you still pay commission to your agent on those fees too, since he did make the original contact, and, of course, he will be able to negotiate the best possible fee for you.

Rates for freelance models at the time of writing are about fourteen to sixteen pounds a day for 'fashion seasons', and around fifteen pounds an hour for photographic work, though daily and weekly rates are usually negotiated between your agent and the client or photographer, and work out at somewhat less than the hourly rate. Money, and the lack of it, is probably the biggest problem you'll have to face when you're starting out on your career. Most agencies prefer you to have some kind of financial backing, either your own savings or your parents' support, to see you through those difficult first few months, because they believe, quite rightly, that it's impossible for a girl to work well if she's desperately worried where next week's rent is coming from. Some agencies will even give you financial help when you're starting – Askew's, for instance, will advance you money, but only if they're convinced that you have real potential and, almost more important, if you are absolutely dedicated to making a career for yourself in modelling. 'We are more careful than we used to be,' says Tony Askew, 'because we found that, with some girls, it didn't help in the long run, because it gave them a false sense of security about money, and the sooner you learn how to manage money when you're self-employed, the better!'

It's very tempting to think, when a long-awaited cheque finally arrives, that it is a kind of bonus, but you must be sensible and realize that it's not only all you have to live on till the next cheque comes in, but also that you'll have to pay National Insurance contributions and Income Tax out of it.

The sensible approach is to put a proportion of every cheque you get into a special bank account so that, when the tax demand comes in, you have the money already there to pay it. There are few things more unpleasant than an unexpected tax demand, when you haven't got the money to pay it.

Don't forget, though, that all the expenses you incur in earning your living – clothes, make-up, hairdressers' bills, taxis – are tax-deductible, provided you can prove that you spent the money, so always ask for a receipt, even if you've only bought a twenty-pence pair of tights. It's a very good idea to make a note of everything you spend in your diary, if not at the time then certainly at the end of each day. It will only take a couple of minutes and will save you a lot of time and trouble trying to remember how much you did spend on 15 October, when the end of the tax year comes round the following April.

Don't think that once you have found yourself an agent, all you have to do is sit back and wait for the work to start pouring in. He will send out your index card – a card with your photograph and details of your measurements on – to all his clients, but you still need to do the rounds, to jog people's memories and to let them see you 'in the flesh'. It's also an opportunity to impress them with your personality, which according to Laraine Ashton, co-founder of Bobton's Agency and now running an agency of her own, accounts for at least fifty per cent of what makes a good model.

Don't forget, either, that although your agent has taken you on, you are only one of twenty or thirty, even seventy girls that he has on his books, and as a newcomer and therefore not a big money-earner yet, you'll need to keep yourself fresh in his mind too, either by dropping into the agency every now and then, or by ringing up every day.

Both Tony Askew and Laraine Ashton believe it's absolutely essential for girls to ring in every afternoon, around five, to see if there is any work for them the following day. 'Obviously, if we have a booking for a girl,' says Laraine, 'we do try and get in touch with her but it isn't always possible, and it's very irritating to have to let a client down at the last minute because we haven't been able to contact the girls he wants to use. Anyway, I think girls should *want* to ring in – I don't see that they can be genuinely interested in their careers if they don't.'

Remember, too, that your agent has been in the business a long time, so be prepared to listen to his advice. 'When girls come in with exceptionally long hair,' says Tony Askew, 'we usually advise them to have it cut a bit, but they don't want to because their boyfriends or mothers don't approve. They start modelling, and though they may be stunning in every other way, the clients don't book them because their hair is dated and not very versatile. Eventually, when they see other girls getting the work they should have been getting, and begin to realize what being professional really means, they'll give in. But they could have avoided all those missed opportunities if only they'd listened!'

Agents are always very busy people, so make sure you don't waste their time. Keep a note-pad and sharpened pencil by the phone so that, when he rings, he doesn't have to hold on while you go and find a piece of paper or sharpen your pencil. Always let him know where you're going to be, so that he doesn't waste time trying to ring you at home if you've gone away for a few days.

Buy yourself a suitable diary and write all your bookings in it as soon as you get them. 'It's inexcusable to miss a job because you threw away the cigarette packet on which you wrote down the details,' says Evelyn Thorsen, 'or to turn up without the right accessories because you didn't make a note of them as soon as you'd put the phone down, and so forgot!'

The qualities that all agents admire in models above all else – including beauty – is professionalism. As Peter Benison says, 'A pretty face is not enough any more!' Tony Askew tells the story of a stunning girl who walked into their offices a couple of years ago, wanting to be a model. 'She was so outstanding that we did something we never normally do, and sent her round to one of the top photographers in the country straightaway. He was so impressed that he wanted to book her exclusively, so we helped to set her up with everything she needed and she started work, but after a few weeks, she suddenly disappeared with a boyfriend and we heard nothing from her for months. Then she turned up at our Milan office saying she was terribly sorry and wanting to start again, so we took her back and she worked well at first, but again, after a few weeks, she disappeared. The next time she turned up saying she was sorry and could she start again, we said no, because we couldn't take the risk. It was a tragedy because she could have been another Shrimpton or Twiggy, but she was just not professional.'

Most agents would define being professional in much the same way – always being on time, always turning up looking well groomed, always having the right accessories, and generally making everyone else's job as easy as you can. Laraine Ashton also believes it's part of a model's job to keep smiling no matter what the circumstances. 'A good model carries everybody else's mood – if the client gets ratty and the photographer gets ratty, it's vital that the model doesn't too, or else the whole session will be a disaster. It is a lot to ask, but the girl who stays good-tempered will always be in demand because people remember that she was fun to work with.'

You should always maintain the highest standards, no matter how badly any of your colleagues behave. 'Unpunctuality and laziness can be catching,' says Peter Benison, 'you may find that a particular photographer is always late for sessions, and it's tempting to think "Oh well, if he isn't going to be there till half past, I won't bother to be either," but don't fall into that trap. His lack of professionalism doesn't justify yours! I always try and drum it into girls to be five or ten minutes early for appointments, and ready to start.'

That isn't to say, though, that you should let yourself be trampled on or bullied by clients or photographers, and a good agent will stand up for your rights and protect you. In return, he will expect you to protect his reputation, not only by being professional and one hundred per cent reliable, but by being polite to clients and not accepting work he doesn't approve of. 'If a girl posed for pornographic photographs or got involved in a scandal,' says Tony Askew, 'then we'd have to ask her to leave. Certain people are only too ready to believe the worst of models and it's unfair to the other girls to subject them to that.' In general, though, your agent will only take you off his books if you are repeatedly unprofessional – missing bookings or turning up late or failing to reach the standard the client reasonably expects of you – or if there is simply a personality clash and it would be better for both sides if you parted company. 'On the few occasions we have had to ask girls to leave,' says Laraine Ashton, 'we have almost always managed to fix them up with another agency – after all, the girl's livelihood is at stake and we wouldn't want to see her unable to work. Oddly enough, though, the difficult girls who we do ask to leave are usually the tough ones who manage to land on their feet anyway!'

Do remember that although you need a good agent if you are going to make a success of your modelling career, he doesn't employ you, and if you feel that he isn't pushing you hard enough or getting you work, then you are free to leave at any time and sign on with another agency, but before you do, it would be worth asking yourself whether you've done everything you can. Have you followed his advice about your appearance or your manner? Have you phoned in every day? Have you always looked your best when you've called in to see him? Have you always been on time for the bookings he's got you and have you always been as professional as you can? You may feel that other girls are being sent to more auditions than you are, but it could be that cool blondes are in demand just then and you're a girl-next-door brunette, so he'd be wasting your time – and the client's – by sending you along. It would also be worth while to have a chat with your agent about the way you feel – he probably won't know unless you tell him, and it could just be a simple misunderstanding that's causing the problems, which could easily be cleared up once it's brought out into the open.

Finally, don't be afraid to go to your agent with any problems you have, whether they're professional or personal. If you're worried or unhappy, then your work will certainly suffer, and since, if you're not making money, your agent won't be getting any commission from you, it is in his interest to give you a shoulder to cry on and whatever practical help he can. You and your agent need each other, and you're united by a common cause – the desire to make your career as successful as it can be.

9 Wholesale modelling

The chances are that, no matter how far your modelling career takes you, it will start in one of the hundreds of wholesale fashion houses in the 'rag trade' district of London – the square mile, roughly, bounded by Oxford Street, Charlotte Street, Euston Road and Portland Place. There you'll find the showrooms of most of the ready-to-wear firms which are household names – John Craig, André Peters, Jinty, Susan Small, Alistaire Cowin – and many more smaller, not so well-known firms, who probably have the biggest share of the wholesale fashion market.

Unless you are outstandingly good – and regardless of how beautiful you may be, it's unlikely that you will be so good when you're starting out – it's in one of these houses that you'll get your first modelling job. The big names in the high fashion, evening wear and young market can have the pick of permanent models – after all, wouldn't you rather be modelling beautiful evening dresses or superbly cut French-style separates than a 'mumsy' Crimplene two-piece? – and so they almost always go for girls who've had some experience. And the only way to get experience is . . . to take a job in one of the lesser-known, middle-of-the-road fashion houses. Once you've come to terms with that fact, it isn't too difficult to find yourself a job as a house model. If you have an agent, then he will arrange interviews for you with suitable houses – no point in going along to see a coat house who want an elegant size twelve, if you're a rather dolly size ten – but if you haven't, and don't mind expending time and energy on a few wild goose chases, you can look for a job yourself. The best place to start is the classified ads in the London evening papers or in those give-away magazines, or you can walk through the 'rag trade' district looking out for signs saying 'Model wanted'. It's also worth calling in at the houses you like the look of and seeing the showroom manageress – she may not have a vacancy just then, but if you're the right size for her clothes and she likes the look of you, then she'll take down your name and address and contact you when a vacancy occurs.

To be a house model, you should be a size 10 or 12, though some firms like a size 14, and a pleasant appearance is more important than striking good looks. The buyers for shops and stores who make up ninety-nine per cent of your audience need to be able to imagine their customers in the clothes you're modelling, and if you are too beautiful or too exotic that might be a little difficult.

Different types of house require different physical characteristics. Bunty, who is showroom manageress at André Peters, who make French-style coats and dresses, always looks for good shoulders, so that the coats sit well, as does Wendy Gordon, till recently with Lionel Norman, another coat house. 'I don't like girls to be too tall, either,' she says. 'Between 5′ 7″ and 5′ 9″ is ideal because you have to remember that most of our coats will wind up on women far closer to the national average of 5′ 3″.'

On the other hand, most evening-wear houses prefer the taller girl because the taller a girl is the more elegant long dresses look on her. Both Bunty and Wendy Gordon avoid girls who are flat-chested. 'Our dresses cave in at the front on a model without a bust,' says Bunty – as does Mac Ridley of Jinty, the young-style dress house: 'A lot of our evening wear have low necklines and it needs a girl with some bosom to show them off to their best advantage.'

Alistaire Cowin, on the other hand, who makes young but rather sophisticated separates, prefers the Twiggy type. 'A flattish chest is important because of the way our clothes are cut and because all our samples are a size 10, and so are good hips since we do a lot of trousers, too. A girl's figure is much more critical with our type of merchandise – in ordinary coat or dress modelling you can cheat quite a bit, pinning things in at the waist or whatever, but with us, it's impossible. Everything has to fit the girl perfectly because it's all on show.'

Once you've got a job as a house model, there are certain basic items you must have. At least two pairs of shoes, for instance – one pair of plain black patent court shoes – for some reason black patent goes with almost everything, whereas black leather doesn't – and another pair in a lighter colour, like beige. If you're working in an evening-wear house, then you'll need a couple of pairs of satin shoes – one white, one black.

Most girls leave their working shoes at work – it saves having to carry them backwards and forwards each day and it also means that you're not tempted to wear them to travel in. It makes more sense to keep your working shoes exclusively for work – that way, they'll stay cleaner, last longer and, perhaps most important, you'll have a cool, unworn pair to slip your tired feet into at the end of a long day.

Some coat houses provide their models with dresses to wear under the coats when they are modelling, but if yours doesn't, then you should have at least one plain round-necked dress, or a matching skirt and sweater, in a neutral colour such as grey, brown or black. Make sure that the skirt is a reasonable length so that there is no chance of it showing beneath the hem of the coats you're displaying.

Most houses don't mind what you wear when you're not showing, provided, of course, you look well groomed and tidy. Some of the more old-fashioned houses do frown on trousers, but others, like Alistaire Cowin, prefer them. 'I'd almost rather see our models in jeans, as long as they're clean and well-cut, because jeans are more our scene than neat little two-pieces!'

Tights should always tone with the clothes you're wearing – darkish brown with winter clothes and dark colours, a flesh colour, or even paler, with summer clothes and light colours. Your tights should tone with your shoes, too – as a general rule, they should never be darker than your shoes. Always carry a spare pair of each shade with you – you never know when you're going to ladder them and you can never afford to let a client see you with laddered tights.

You'll need a variety of underwear, too, depending on what kind of house you're working in. In general you should always have a spare flesh-coloured set if you're wearing white and vice versa, and never wear black underwear to work unless you are certain that you will only be modelling thick winter coats. If you're working in a dress or separates house, then you should have a black bra and briefs with you in case you have to model something dark and vaguely see-through, and in an evening-wear house you'll need a strapless bra, and perhaps a halter-necked, or low-backed one, too.

It's a good idea to keep a set of essential make-up at work – foundation, blusher, eyeshadow, mascara, lipstick – to save you carrying your entire make-up kit backwards and forwards every day.

Wholesale modelling isn't a particularly glamorous occupation, and your surroundings are unlikely to be very elegant. In the smaller houses, the showroom also doubles up as reception area and office, and more likely than not your changing room will also be the stock room, though in the larger ones the accommodation is likely to be more luxurious. As a house model, your job first and foremost is to sell clothes, not to provide a glamorous afternoon's entertainment for the general public, and you are very directly involved in the process of selling. When you step out into the showroom, your sole purpose is to persuade as many buyers in the room as you can to place an order for the garment you're modelling. As you model, you tell them the style number of your outfit and its wholesale price, usually about half what the garment will sell at in the shops. It's not a bad idea to remind yourself of what a customer will eventually pay for the outfit you're wearing – it isn't a £20 coat, it's a £40 one – and model it accordingly!

In the bigger, more traditional houses, if the buyers like the garment they will give you a small plastic ring from the wooden stand in front of them – a different colour for each buyer – and when you go back into the changing room, you slip all the rings you've been given for that particular garment over the hook of its coat-hanger, so that after the show you will know which buyers want to have a closer look at which garments. From your point of view, the more rings you collect the better because it shows that you are really selling the garments you're modelling. You might think that most garments sell themselves and the way you model them has very little to do with whether the buyers order them or not, but you'd be wrong. 'Models are *so* important,' says Bunty of André Peters. 'You can have the best coat or suit in the world, but a bad model can kill it stone dead! We've had occasions where one particular outfit wasn't selling at all, but before we took it out of the collection, we thought we'd just try it on another girl. She walked out into the showroom in it and collected rings from all over the room!'

Once the show is over, you'll be expected to help get the garments ready on the rail for the buyers to inspect more closely. All the garments with a red ring go on to one rail, all those with a blue ring go on to another, all those with an orange ring go on to yet another, and so on. If a garment has several different rings, then place it on one buyer's rail first and when he or she has finished looking at it, pass it on to the next buyer who gave it a ring.

As a house model, you could be called upon to model clothes at any time, but the vast majority of your modelling will be done during the 'seasons' – periods of between four and six weeks in April/May and October/November when the autumn and spring collections respectively are shown to the buyers and the Press. Some of the younger houses such as Jinty and Alistaire Cowin are breaking down the season system by showing more or less continually throughout the year and using only their house models to show the clothes, but the majority of houses still follow the traditional pattern and take on anything from a couple to a dozen or more freelance girls during the seasons, since there may be anything up to two hundred and fifty garments to be shown in two or three set shows, or even more spur-of-the-moment shows, in the course of a day. Some of the big, more exclusive houses don't use their house model for the seasons unless she's very experienced, but the vast majority do and some will even pay you a bit extra during those four or five weeks, as you'll be working so much harder than usual.

During a season, professionalism is absolutely vital. There may be six of you changing in and out of twenty different outfits in a room the size of your bedroom, so it is essential to be tidy and to keep your things where you can find them in a hurry. Whether or not you have a dresser to help you, there is no excuse for throwing your clothes on the floor as you step out of them.

Remember that, in almost every case, what you're showing is the only sample of that particular garment and it has got to stay looking good for the whole four or six weeks if anyone is going to order it.

You will have to learn self-discipline too – your first season is very exciting and while there is no reason why you shouldn't enjoy it, don't get over-excited. Wendy Gordon remembers a season where she felt as though she was 'running a kindergarten not a showroom, with five girls all sitting round giggling non-stop!' They may have enjoyed themselves but it didn't create a very good impression on either the customers or the staff, and the freelance girls involved weren't booked again.

When you are just starting out, a season is a marvellous opportunity to learn, not only from experience, but from the other girls, most of whom are extremely professional – they have to be or they simply wouldn't survive as freelancers. Don't be overawed by them, though – remember that they probably started in the same sort of job you're in – or afraid to ask their advice. Although some of them may seem very aloof, even hard, the vast majority are only too glad to pass on any tips they can to a newcomer.

The seasons, though, only take up eight, or at most ten, weeks of the year, and although you may be asked to show the odd garment to a buyer out of season, the majority of the time you'll either be down at the factory, having the clothes for next season's collection fitted on you, or in the showroom, helping out generally, writing price tickets for garments, covering them in polythene ready for dispatch, typing, invoicing, even making the tea. Alistaire Cowin expects his house model not only to have a perfect figure, but also to be intelligent, to be interested in the firm's merchandise, to have a good telephone manner, since she doubles up as switchboard operator, and to have a pleasant manner with the customers, since she doubles up as receptionist too.

Like any office job, wholesale modelling, for forty weeks a year when you're not showing, is very much what you make it. If you choose to do only the bare minimum, you may well find that time drags and you get very bored. But if you take a real interest in the clothes your company is making, and make the most of your opportunity to learn about fashion, about fabrics, cut, and colour co-ordination, you're not only gaining valuable knowledge that will help you in your modelling career, you're also acquiring the kind of experience that could lead ultimately to a job in the fashion world, perhaps as a showroom manageress, later on.

As a wholesale model, your showroom manageress is the most important person in your working life, and though some of them have reputations for being real dragons, the majority are only concerned with keeping their showroom running smoothly, and as long as you help to make their job easier, you'll stay on the right side of them. In every single case, their major grumble about models is unpunctuality. 'I dislike girls who arrive at nine o'clock without their make-up on,' says Wendy Gordon. 'If they want to arrive at twenty to, and put it on here, I don't mind at all, but they must be ready to start at nine.'

The top of the tree as far as permanent modelling jobs go are the *haute couture* salons, for example, Dior, Cardin, and St Laurent in Paris, Hardy Amies, John Cavanagh and Norman Hartnell in London. Financially, you wouldn't be much better off, especially when you're just starting, but you would be working in beautiful surroundings – plush carpeted, mirrored rooms hung with chandeliers – showing superbly made clothes in exquisite fabrics to rich, often famous, and sometimes even beautiful women.

Because the jobs are so sought after, and so few and far between – Hartnell, for instance, only employs three full-time models – the standard is extremely high. 'We look for girls who are at the very least 5′ 8″,' says Mara, chief model at Hartnell, 'with good bones, in their bodies as well as their faces – the clothes need the right frame to show them at their best – and with superb legs, ideally, long from the knee to the ankle. Mr Hartnell likes girls to have a very distinctive hair colouring – very dark or very fair or a striking redhead – and hair that is long enough to put up. We also look for that certain something, an elegance, a sense of style, an awareness of the clothes she's wearing which is impossible to define, but we know it when we see it!'

If you've set your heart on a career in *haute couture*, the best way, Mara says, to get there is to take a permanent job in a good wholesale house for a year or so, then try your hand at freelance work to polish off any remaining rough edges. 'That isn't to say, though, that we wouldn't take on a girl with no experience if we thought she had the makings of a good model. In that case, she would start as a receptionist, and perhaps model the occasional garment – the bride's dress, if there was one in the collection – but it would be a couple of years before she would be modelling full-time or showing to private clients.'

Whichever way you started, though, you would spend some time learning to model in the style your couturier likes. Some like their girls to move quickly and smoothly to give movement to their clothes, others prefer the more traditional, rather languid way of moving. At Hartnell, the style of modelling is very simple, no fussy hand movements, no complicated turns, nothing that will detract from the clothes. Like the wholesale houses, *haute couture* salons do most of their showing during the seasons – January and July in their case, rather than April and October – though the models do quite a lot of showing to individual clients who come in to have another look at the outfit they are thinking of ordering.

As an *haute couture* model, you also spend infinitely more time being fitted – sixty hours of fittings for one garment isn't unusual! If you're a wholesale model, then the garment being fitted on you will be the pattern for every size 10 or 12 that's produced, so if, for instance, your left shoulder was marginally higher than your right, it can't be made to fit you exactly – it would be absurd to produce two thousand coats with the left shoulder slightly higher than the right, since ninety-nine per cent of the women who'll buy them have perfectly level shoulders. In an *haute couture* salon, every client who orders the dress you're modelling has it made specifically to her own measurements, and since it's very unlikely that anyone will buy the dress you actually show in the collection, it can be made to fit you perfectly. And that takes time, but, Mara points out, you need a lot of patience if you're going to be a successful model. 'It's one of my talents – I can stand for hours and not mind at all, though I must say if you're being fitted for a thick, tweed winter coat in the middle of a July heatwave, it can be a little uncomfortable!' A really good model inspires her couturier – for instance, Norman Hartnell usually designs slightly more extrovert clothes in vibrant colours on Mara because they go so well with her very distinctive colouring.

What with all the private showings and the fittings, there isn't much spare time, and you wouldn't be expected to do anything more arduous than write out invitation cards for the shows, or possibly stand in for the receptionist while she's at lunch.

Once you've managed to get a job in an *haute couture* house, you may well choose to stay there for the rest of your modelling career, but many of the girls who take permanent jobs in wholesale houses see it only as a short-term measure before they go freelance.

The best time to take the plunge is a few weeks before either of the seasons, when the demand for freelance models is at its height and there are barely enough girls to go round – a lot of photographic models do the seasons, because you're always paid in cash at the end of each week, and if you're waiting months for fees from photographic work to come in, a little ready money can come in very useful.

Your agent will sort out the most suitable houses for you to go and see – again, it would be a waste of everybody's time if you went along to auditions for which you were totally unsuitable – and it shouldn't take more than a couple of interviews before you get a booking. Do go along prepared – the showroom manageress will almost certainly want to see you in some of her garments and will definitely want to see you walk. 'It never fails to amaze me,' says Bunty of André Peters, 'how many girls turn up for an audition in those great clumpy shoes that they cannot possibly model in, without even bringing a pair of court shoes with them. We can provide her with a pair of shoes, but to me the fact that she hasn't bothered to bring her own shows that she hasn't got the right attitude.'

As a freelance model, you're paid considerably more than a house model – you'd earn in two days what she earns in a week – although do remember that it's only for eight or possibly ten weeks of the year. Since you cost a house a lot of money, you're expected to be worth the extra in every way. 'My ideal show model,' says Bunty, 'has an extremely good walk, good shoulders and a well-proportioned size 10 figure, which does create problems, since girls who are slim enough on the hips tend to be flat-chested, which isn't ideal for showing dresses. I go for good-looking rather than pretty girls, but I don't like them aloof or cold. Although the buyers are mainly looking at the garment, they can't help noticing faces and their over-all impression of how the garment looks is affected by the expression on a girl's face. If she looks hard and bitter they tend not to go for the outfit, but if she looks as though she's enjoying wearing it, they'll buy it.'

Naturally, you're expected to be able to change very quickly because nothing looks worse than gaps in a show – they throw the other models, irritate the customers, and drive showroom manageresses to distraction, so it's unlikely that they'll book you again. But if you prove yourself to be a thorough professional, you'll find the same firm booking you season after season. 'It makes my job easier,' says Wendy Gordon, 'and the customers like it, especially the ones who are a bit shy, because they recognize the faces and it makes them feel more at home somehow.'

There is, according to people on both sides of the fence, nothing like the amount of bitchiness in modelling that there is supposed to be. 'On the rare occasions that you do get a bitchy girl,' says Wendy Gordon, 'the others very quickly sort her out. Anyway, when I'm booking girls, I always look for pleasant faces – I avoid very hard or sulky ones like the plague.'

The pinnacle for freelance girls, though, are not the seasons, but the prestige shows held by big stores such as Harrods and Selfridges, or by groups of designers such as Bill Gibb and Gina Fratini, and Zandra Rhodes. They are the most glamorous, and the most highly paid, so the competition is very fierce. It's not unusual to find at least a hundred other girls at an audition. That's when you need to preserve your self-confidence at all costs. If you tell yourself that you don't stand a chance against the others, then you won't, but if you believe that you are every bit as good as they are, you'll stand an extremely good chance of being chosen.

Most big shows these days are produced more like a musical than a fashion show, with several days' rehearsal beforehand, and it's rare to find yourself simply modelling. You'll probably be asked to dance your way along the catwalk or across the stage to a routine worked out for you by a choreographer. It is very hard work, but try to remember it's also great fun. At one big fashion show recently, presented around the swimming pool of a smart hotel just outside London, one of the most beautiful girls in the show did herself less than justice because she was frowning with concentration as she danced, and silently mouthing 'One-two-three-four!' as she tried to remember each step.

Shows like these really put your professionalism to the test – you'll probably be expected to show twenty or thirty different outfits, with only a couple of minutes to change, alter your hairstyle if necessary, get together the accessories you need between each outfit, and to emerge each time looking as though you've just spent an hour getting ready.

The standards demanded are probably the highest in any sphere of freelance show modelling, but then so are the rewards, and not only the financial ones. 'There is no bigger thrill,' says Viscountess Davidson, a top model for many years and until her recent marriage principal of the London Academy of Modelling, 'than modelling beautiful clothes to a big, enthusiastic audience. It's the same sort of exhilaration an actress must get from knowing she can twist an audience round her little finger. For me, that's what modelling was all about.'

10 A day in the life of a wholesale model

For Hendrika, a twenty-four-year-old South African girl who is the house model at Dennis Siegal, a small coat house in Eastcastle Street, in the heart of London's rag trade district, there is no such thing as *a* typical day – there are several. First, there are the days during the four or six weeks of the seasons, in April and May, and October/November, when Hendrika is in perpetual motion from nine till five showing about a hundred garments along with three or four freelance girls taken on for the season. And since the firm doesn't do set shows, they show the range to the buyers as they arrive and it could be anything up to eight times a day. Each show can take anything up to forty-five minutes, so by the time Hendrika has helped to sort out the coats that the buyers have 'ringed' on to their respective rails, helped the showroom manageress take the orders by reading out the stock numbers and the wholesale prices of each garment from the tickets, it's time to start work again, often without even time for a cup of tea or a chance to sit down. But whatever the time of year, Hendrika's day always begins in the same way.

7.00 am   The alarm clock goes off, and she gets straight out of bed – she's got her morning routine worked out down to the last second and she knows that an extra few minutes in bed may well mean that she misses her train. She switches on her heated rollers, then sets her hair and leaves the rollers in while she does her make-up. 'That takes between twenty minutes and half an hour, and I have to do it thoroughly because I just don't have time to retouch it during the day, especially during the seasons. I know a lot of girls do their faces on the train or wait till they get into work, but I can never be sure that I'll get a seat, and it isn't easy to put make-up on standing up. I don't like leaving it till I get in either, just in case I've got a customer at nine.'

7.45   She gets dressed, takes the heated rollers out of her hair and combs it into shape, then drinks a glass of hot water with a slice of lemon in it and eats a bowl of cornflakes, before dashing off to Kew Station to catch the

8.15. This morning she's lucky and gets a seat. At Victoria she changes on to the Victoria line – no seat this time, as the train is packed – and arrives at Oxford Circus about five to nine. Luckily the showroom is only two or three minutes' walk, so she's in the office by nine.

9.00   This morning only one buyer is coming in, and then not till half past ten, so Hendrika doesn't bother to change into the plain round-necked jersey dress that the firm provides for her, and the plain black patent court shoes she keeps at work, and goes straight to the switchboard – one of the jobs she does when she isn't modelling. 'Outside the seasons, boredom is the biggest problem,' she admits. 'I do take an interest in the clothes and have learnt a lot about fabrics and styling and colour co-ordination since I've been here, but there are days when my boss hasn't even got the odd letter for me to type, so apart from looking after the switchboard there really is nothing for me to do. The other slight problem was that there wasn't anyone else of my own age in the firm – the only other woman, the showroom manageress, is old enough to be my mother, and though we get on very well it's not like having someone your own age to talk to. But then a week ago I heard that they've taken on another girl who's about twenty, to help out – she'll be starting next week and I'm rather looking forward to it.'

10.15   Hendrika goes into the stockroom, which also serves as a dressing-room, and slips into her working dress and shoes.

10.25   She goes into the tiny kitchen, lays out a tray and puts on the kettle for some coffee. 'I don't always make the coffee or tea – it just depends on who's busy. The showroom manageress is on the phone at the moment so I'm doing it, but if I'd been tied up with a customer, then she would have done it. During the seasons it's not a problem either – somehow we always seem to get freelance girls who don't mind lending a hand in that way, but I do know of girls who would think it was beneath their dignity.'

10.30   The buyer arrives – she owns her own shop in a small Home Counties town and couldn't get along to see the winter range when it was shown in April/May. First of all, Hendrika goes through the rails of winter coats with her, pointing out which particular garments have been selling well, to try and help her decide which garments she wants to see modelled. The woman examines each coat very carefully and it's a slow process. 'You usually find that the buyers from small shops are a lot more fussy about what they'll buy. For one thing, they know their customers very well, and know exactly what sort of coats will sell, whereas a buyer from a big store or a chain of shops is trying to cater for all types of customer, and so can take a bit of a chance, and for another they've only got a limited amount of money to spend.'

10.50 The buyer has chosen eight coats from the range that she would like Hendrika to model. She takes them into the stockroom/dressing-room and slips into the first one, in a beige and brown check. She does up the buttons, ties the tie belt loosely in the front, checks in the full-length mirror that her skirt isn't showing underneath the coat and the collar is lying perfectly flat at the back, then walks out into the showroom. The buyer and the showroom manageress are sitting together, with a folder in front of them, giving the style number, details of the fabric used, and swatches of the different colours the coats come in, so all Hendrika has to do is quote the wholesale price and model the garment as well as she can. She walks towards the buyer and away from her, and does a full turn to show off the fullness of the coat, then goes back into the dressing-room to change into the next one. As there is only one customer today, they have dispensed with rings – the customer merely tells the showroom manageress which coats she'll order. 'I really love modelling. I enjoy wearing clothes I wouldn't be able to afford myself and getting buyers to order them.'

11.20 Hendrika finishes modelling the last coat, then puts them all on a rail and wheels it out into the showroom. The buyer has decided to order seven of the eight coats. The only one she doesn't want is the one that Hendrika liked best, because it was one of the younger styles – but most of her customers are middle-aged, and she knows there wouldn't be much chance of selling it. Hendrika reads out the style numbers and wholesale price on each ticket as the showroom manageress writes down the order, and when that's finished, takes the coats and replaces them, in order, on the rail.

11.55 The buyer finally leaves – 'It always seems to take much longer when there's only one,' she says. 'I suppose it's because they chat more.' She washes up the coffee cups, changes out of her working clothes, and goes back to the switchboard for half an hour.

12.30 pm She slips out for a sandwich and a cup of coffee – 'I have to be a little bit careful about eating too much stodge, but I'm fairly lucky in that I don't put on weight too easily' – and a quick look round Top Shop to see what's new. There are a couple of dresses she likes, but she's just had to pay her share of the telephone bill, so there isn't any point even in trying them on.

1.30   Back to the office, where her boss is waiting to take her to the factory in Kentish Town for a fitting session. Usually they go in the morning, but today it hasn't been possible. This aspect of the rag trade is usually far from glamorous and this factory, like so many others, is a big, dark, almost Dickensian building housing a lot of rag trade firms, although the inside is much more airy, more pleasant than the outside would lead you to expect.

2.00   There are a dozen or more coats ready for fitting. They are cut from a pattern, made up, and only then tried on Hendrika to make sure that they fit properly. This is the first fitting for the spring range, so everybody involved – Hendrika's boss, the managing director of the firm, the cloth buyer, the designer, and the cutter – is there. There are no problems with the first coat, but the second one that she tries on is longer at the front than at the back. Hendrika turns round so that everyone can see the gently sloping hem line. The cutter adjusts the coat on her shoulders, but that makes no difference to the way it hangs, so he gets out the pins and begins to adjust the hem. As he works, the others discuss his progress and Hendrika just stands. 'I'm like a dummy during fittings,' she says. 'They talk about the coat and the way it fits on the shoulders or across the back as though I'm not there, but I don't mind – I've got used to it!'

3.00   The third coat needs only a small adjustment to the positioning of the buttons. 'Do you like it, Hendrika?' the managing director asks. 'If you saw it on sale in a shop for forty pounds would you buy it?' She looks at herself in the mirror. 'No, I wouldn't,' she says after some thought. 'I think it's a nice coat and it would look good on someone of my mother's age, but it's too old for me.' She is always honest when they ask her opinion of a garment, as she says there is no point in being anything else, since they genuinely want to know what she thinks and they aren't going to sack her if she doesn't like every coat.

4.00   No problem with the next two coats, and while they are all discussing why the shoulders of the sixth coat aren't sitting properly, someone brings the tea. Since the cutter is making adjustments to the coat she's wearing, Hendrika can't drink hers, although she's dying for a cup. 'Sometimes, if it's very hectic, I don't get a chance to drink it at all, and I just have to stand and look at it getting colder and colder.'

4.30   Hendrika tries on another four coats, all of which fit pretty well, and only minor adjustments are needed. By the time five o'clock comes round, Hendrika's feet are killing her and she gratefully accepts a lift from her boss back to Oxford Circus, where she battles her way on to a train.

6.15 She gets back to the flat, and after a ten-minute sit down, she starts to cook her supper, her main meal of the day. Two nights a week, she goes to modern dance classes which she enjoys and which help to keep her figure in good shape, but not tonight. 'It's just as well – I don't think I'd have had the strength anyway.' Instead she washes her hair, does a bit of washing and irons the shirt she wants to wear next morning.

9.00 She sits down to watch television for a while, and gives herself a manicure at the same time. By ten-thirty, she's getting ready for bed. 'I have to be in bed by eleven – I really do need eight hours' sleep if I'm going to cope with work the next day. If I do go out with my boyfriend and have a late night during the week, then I go to bed very early the following night to catch up on the sleep I missed.'

11.00 Hendrika is in bed, asleep.

11 Photographic modelling

Appearing on the cover of *Vogue* is to the modelling world what topping the bill at the London Palladium is to showbusiness, and though in both cases it may sometimes seem like 'overnight' success, it's usually taken not only talent, but years of determination and sheer hard work to get there.

The photographic side of modelling is what most girls have in mind when they set their hearts on careers as models, partly because it seems the most glamorous side of the business – how the Jean Shrimptons and Twiggies of this world made their fortunes and became household names – and partly because it's the only area most of us have any contact with. After all, everybody sees posters and flips through magazines where models are featured in the advertisements and on the fashion and beauty pages, but very few of us ever see models working in wholesale fashion houses or top couturiers' salons, modelling garments for clients.

But once you've done your model training and have had some experience of showroom work, you may decide that you prefer working to a live audience or discover that you just aren't very photogenic, though in all probability, like most girls, you'll still have your sights set on the cover of *Vogue*.

Like so many other 'glamorous' professions where the rewards are high – a top photographic model can earn up to twenty thousand pounds a year – the competition is extremely fierce, and the myth about the girl being stopped in the street by the famous photographer who gasps 'That face – it's what I've been looking for all these years!' is just that, a myth, or possibly the Candid Camera team up to their tricks again.

Getting your first break into photographic modelling takes time, energy and money, and your agent may well suggest you take a permanent job in a showroom or do the seasons, partly to make sure you've got enough money coming in to pay the rent and partly to give you enough time to save what you'll need to launch yourself on a photographic career.

No doubt about it, it's an expensive business. Apart from the make-up, wigs, hair-pieces, accessories – four or five pairs of decent shoes, for instance, in different styles and colours – you'll need a portfolio, a slim zip-up case with a dozen or so polythene folders attached inside and, of course, enough good photographs to fill it.

You might think that any top photographer could tell just by looking at your face how well you'll photograph, but that isn't the case, as Barry Lategan, one of the most successful photographers in fashion and advertising today, points out. 'I still can't tell from the first glance at a girl as she walks through the door whether or not she's photogenic. I know there are supposed to be rules about bone-structure and faces being in proportion – equal distances between hairline, eyebrows, nose and chin – but I don't honestly think they apply. Look at Jean Shrimpton – her retroussé nose means that the balance of her face is wrong according to the rules – and look at Twiggy with that high forehead and long neck. As far as I'm concerned, it's the *unusual* features, the ones that don't conform, that make a really outstanding face.'

Since a photographer may well decide whether or not to book you on the strength of your portfolio photographs, they've obviously got to show you at your very best, and though it's tempting when you're starting out to try and save some money by letting Uncle George, who's a very keen amateur photographer, do them for you, it won't start your career off on the right foot.

'Any professional photographer can spot an amateur's work a mile off,' says Peter Noble, an advertising photographer whose clients include Innoxa make-up and Maxwell Croft furs, 'and a portfolio full of it will give him the wrong impression about you. You're a professional, too, and that's the image you want to put across from the start. The same is true of the local photographer in the High Street. Although he earns his living taking photographs, the majority of his work is weddings, baby pictures and the golf club dinner-dance, so you can't expect him to be able to produce top-class fashion shots. A Mini is an excellent little car, but you wouldn't enter one for the Monaco Grand Prix, would you?'

So the photographer you want to take your portfolio pictures will almost certainly be based in London, earning his living in fashion or advertising – your agent will have a list of names and will probably be able to recommend a good few from personal experience – and there are two ways to approach it. If your agent knows a photographer well, he may be able to arrange for you to get some test shots done – the photographer may want to try out a new camera or a new type of film, or an idea for a fashion spread he's been commissioned to do, and wants to experiment a little before he goes off to shoot it. You won't get paid, but in return for your time, you may be given a sheet of contacts – small prints of every shot he took. He may well mark the ones he likes, but that could be because his idea has worked out well, not because they show you at your best. The most sensible idea is to look at them with your agent, and though obviously you can pick out the ones you like best – probably the ones that flatter you, because after all you're only human – the final decision ought to be his. He knows the business inside out, and from experience can tell which shots are most likely to appeal to a potential client.

Once you've decided between you on the half a dozen or so that you like, the photographer will sell you blow-ups – large prints, usually fifteen inches by twelve – at around two pounds each. The advantages of getting your pictures done that way are obvious – a few pounds for a portfolio of photographs isn't expensive – but there are disadvantages. For one thing, the session is for the photographer's benefit, not yours, so you won't have much say in the type of shots he does, and for another, all the pictures will show you in the same outfit, probably projecting the same image.

The other way is to commission a photographer to do your portfolio for you, and since you'll be spending up to fifty pounds, it's essential to find a photographer you like, who makes you feel at ease in what will, at first, be the unfamiliar, rather frightening surroundings of a photographic studio, and it's well worth shopping around till you find him.

'It's very hard to walk into anywhere "cold" and do your best pictures,' says Grace Coddington, former top model and now one of *Vogue*'s fashion editors, 'and if the photographer makes you feel positively uneasy, it's even worse!' So spend some time talking to the photographer, see whether you're on the same wavelength, and if there's anything about him that disturbs you – maybe something as simple as the fact that he's got red hair and you've never liked men with red hair – then thank him for his time and trouble, say you'll think about it, and try somebody else.

When you've found the right photographer for you, and before you go along for the session, look through a variety of magazines to get some idea of the kind of picture you want, and how best you can project your image. If you and your agent think you're the slinky, glamorous type, there's no point in being photographed in old jeans, riding a bike. Beware of copying any idea too closely, though – nobody's interested in a second Twiggy or another Vivienne Lynn. What you want to get across is *you*, your individuality and what it is that makes you that all-important bit different from all the other models around.

In practical terms, what you'd expect to get from a session are some head shots – close-ups of your face – some full-length shots that show your figure and legs to advantage, and shots of any special feature, your hands or hair for instance, which you think might be good enough to get you specialist work such as nail polish or shampoo advertisements.

Again, after the session you'll get several sheets of contacts, and again with your agent's help, you'll pick the best half dozen or so for your portfolio – this time the blow-ups are free, included in the price of the session – possibly one for the agency's head sheet, a large poster with photographs of all the girls on their books, with whom you share the cost of producing it, and two or maybe three for your all-important index card.

On it are your measurements, in inches and centimetres, your dress, glove and shoe sizes, the colour of your hair and eyes, and any special ability you have – riding, swimming, driving for instance – printed in both English and German or French, as there's a lot of work for English models in Europe these days, and two or three photographs – at least one head shot and one full length.

When you're starting your career, your cards will be in black and white, and will cost roughly twenty to thirty pounds for a thousand cards, though obviously rates vary, but once you're working regularly and have more money to spend, you can have your cards printed in colour.

In any case, it's essential that you keep your cards up to date and accurate, since in the beginning, anyway, photographers and fashion editors will probably book you on the strength of it. If you start your career with long blonde hair, then after a few months cut it very short and dye it red, you must have new cards with new pictures printed, or, if the change is less drastic, make sure that your old ones are altered accordingly. If you are booked by a photographer as a blonde and you arrive as a red-head, not only will you lose your fee, it will harm your agency's reputation; and though it's yet to happen, the photographer could, under the contract drawn up between the Association of London Model Agencies and the Association of Fashion, Advertising and Editorial Photographers, expect you to make up for the time and money you've cost him.

It's important, too, to keep your portfolio up to date – once you've started working, you'll probably be given a blow-up, free, if you ask, from every session you do, and of course you'll want to include photographs of yourself from magazines or newspapers, the proof that you are indeed a working model.

Once your index cards have been printed, your agent will send them out to everybody – fashion and beauty editors, photographers, advertising agencies – who might want to use you, but that doesn't mean you can simply sit back and wait for the bookings to pour in. In the first week or so, someone might notice you as a new face and give you work right away, but more than likely your card will be filed away with all the others, and, unless you do something about it, forgotten.

The only way you can ensure that doesn't happen is to start on what most people consider the toughest part of a model's job – doing the rounds of magazine offices, studios and agencies to show people your portfolio and yourself. Your agent will give you a list of some two thousand names, and though the most important ones will be marked, even going to see all of those is a pretty daunting prospect, or can be if you don't go about it in the right way.

From talking to established models, the best system seems to be to buy yourself an *A to Z* of London, then divide all the names on your list into postal districts. On Monday, for instance, you could concentrate on seeing people in the W1 area, on Tuesday, SW3, on Wednesday, WC2, and so on, which means that you wouldn't be spending hours on buses and tubes dashing backwards and forwards across London. In theory, it's best to phone first and try and make an appointment, but busy people may put you off, so since you're planning to be in the area anyway, risk just dropping in. If the person you want to see is out or tied up, then you can make a firm appointment for another time. Try to stick fairly rigidly to your districts – if a photographer in WC2 can't see you on the Wednesday you call, but could fit you in the following Monday, when you plan to be in W1, then thank him nicely but try and arrange an appointment for your next WC2 day, otherwise you'll be defeating the object of your careful planning, and be dashing about, wasting time, money and energy. Don't be too disappointed if you turn up for a firm appointment and find the person you've come to see isn't there. If a job has come up at the last minute, you can't really expect a photographer to turn down several hundred pounds' worth of work, just because he's arranged to see you.

Remember too, that first impressions are important – if you arrive for an interview looking as though you've just crawled out of bed, you won't exactly inspire confidence in the person you've come to see. Don't forget that he or she is seeing dozens of girls every week, so anything you can do – on the plus side, of course – to make yourself stand out from the crowd will help. Peter Noble remembers vividly one girl who decorated her portfolio with pressed wild flowers – of course it made no difference at all to her ability as a model, but she stuck in his mind, and when he needed that type of girl, she was the first one he thought of.

On the whole, people try to be polite and kind to models, particularly to new girls. 'If a girl isn't right for us,' said *Woman's* fashion editor, Billie Figg, 'then I do try and explain why, though it can be extremely difficult. If there's something specific that can be put right – her hair may be too long, or the style too freaky, then I'll tell her that, and leave her to decide whether she wants to do anything about it.'

Both Barry Lategan and Grace Coddington find it difficult to give advice to new girls. 'It's such a matter of personal taste,' Barry Lategan says, 'and even now I wouldn't like to say to any girl that she isn't going to make it as a model. Take Twiggy. In her case, she was obviously very photogenic, but no-one could foresee the stroke of luck – Deidre McSharry saying in the *Daily Express* that this was the face of '66 – that really got her career off to such a flying start.'

What they both will do, though, is try and stop a girl from making herself into a carbon copy of anyone else. 'Often girls come in saying they've been advised to have their teeth capped or all their hair cut off,' says Grace Coddington, 'and I usually try to talk them out of it because they'll lose all their individuality and that's the most valuable asset they've got. I don't want to use girls who look like somebody else.'

But detailed, constructive advice takes the kind of time that busy photographers and fashion editors haven't got to spare, and so they may seem off-hand or brusque, but that's something you'll have to learn to take in your stride. 'The biggest problem that faces any girl starting out,' Barry Lategan believes, 'is keeping her confidence intact. It's very hard for the first six months or so, traipsing round, showing people her book and being rejected, especially as people in this business have a habit of making everything seem like a fault. "She's *too* tall," they say, "She's *too* sad looking," or "She looks *too* cheeky," as though any of those things in themselves were defects in the girl. What she's got to keep telling herself is "They've rejected an image, they haven't rejected *me*!" Could be they wanted a blonde and she's a brunette, or a girl with a round face when hers is oval . . .'

You've also got to remember that the people you're going to see are only human, and have strongly developed personal tastes. Barry Lategan, for instance, goes for soft, romantic, 'grown-up Alice in Wonderland-looking' girls, like Ingrid Boulting or Helga Jones, while Niké Williams, fashion editor of *Honey*, finds that kind of beauty 'dribbly looking, and pasty faced'. 'I go for girls with very strong, forceful faces – at the moment I have this thing about cats, and the girls I'm using now are rather busty and look like cats, with slanting eyes and very sexy looks. Slightly odd faces attract me – girls with crooked noses, or overbleached hair for example. I dare say they aren't the man-in-the-street's idea of models, but that's the kind of look I like.' Niké is known to be fairly demanding to work for – she herself admits it – and at a recent session had the model with her face painted blue swinging from a trapeze. At another, Shirley Anne, who's been modelling very successfully for almost ten years and whom Niké uses quite often, spent an afternoon in a chilly underground car park dressed in a sweater, tights, ankle-high boots and a cotton duster coat while a wind-machine blew cold air up the coat to get the effect Niké was after.

Niké's one of the few people in the business to use girls she meets at parties or comes across serving in shops – Josephine Florent, one of the fastest-rising young models around, was working in the Jean Machine in Chelsea when Niké found her – and when she does use an established model, her first thought is how she can change her image. 'There's one girl who does a lot of dreamy, romantic commercials, and when she came in to see me, I said "Can't use you, you pasty-faced thing, you!", but then I thought "Yes I can", so I changed her hairstyle completely, and got her crawling along a bar on all fours like a cat, and she absolutely loved it because no-one had ever asked her to do anything like it before. I'm sure that now people see she can look different, they'll use her in the way I did, too.'

If a fashion editor or photographer sees you in a way that you've never seen yourself, it's certainly worth giving it a try – as long as it doesn't involve doing anything too drastic like shaving all your hair off or having your face tattooed, of course – and a whole new look can give even established models a new lease of professional life.

Grace Coddington, on *Vogue*, tends to work with one or maybe two models more or less exclusively for as long as six months at a time. 'At the moment it's Marie Helvin [David Bailey's latest protégé and wife] who's half-German, half-Japanese. When she was first booked, it was mainly for her oriental looks, but now I use her because I think she's just a fantastic-looking girl – beautiful face, lovely skin, perfect figure, good legs . . . If I like a girl that much, I mould the look around her, and she influences very strongly the clothes I choose to put her in.'

For Billie Figg, of *Woman*, the most important quality, apart from physical basics such as perfect teeth and nice eyes, is likeability. 'Our readers have got to *like* the girl, and want to look like her, not hate her guts because she's so impossibly beautiful. There are certain girls I wouldn't use because they're beautiful in a way that our readers can't identify with – very cold, unapproachable beauties.'

Since tastes do vary so much and cover virtually the whole spectrum, your perseverance will almost inevitably pay off in the end. You'll be exactly what someone is looking for, and you'll get that magical first booking.

Naturally you'll arrive at the studio on time and ready made-up, or early enough to get your face and your hair done before the session is due to start. 'Oh, the gratitude, joy and surprise you feel,' says Billie Figg, 'when you've booked a girl for nine o'clock, and though you've had to slip off to organize a location or sort out the photographer's problems, she's actually gone ahead and got herself ready, instead of waiting till everybody is assembled, then starting.'

Punctuality is one of the cardinal virtues in a model – everyone in the fashion business stresses how important it is and bewails the fact that, although every model has it drummed into her while she's training, all too many girls arrive late. 'In advertising especially,' says Peter Noble, 'every minute costs money, and the girl who's late is not only wasting my time, she's wasting the time of the other models, the make-up artists, the client . . . At worst, the girl would be made to pay for everybody else's time, and at best, I'd think very hard before I ever booked her again.'

If you have to cancel a session you've been booked for, you *must* give the photographer at least twenty-four hours' notice through your agent so that a replacement can be found in time. If you don't, you will rapidly get a reputation for unreliability and neither the photographer nor his client will risk booking you again.

Apart from being on time, Barry Lategan expects his models to arrive with clean hair, unblemished skin and looking fresh. 'If a girl turns up looking spotty and as though she hasn't bothered to get a good night's sleep, then she's unprofessional and shows that she hasn't got the same integrity towards the picture that I have. I know everybody has their off-days, but top photographic models just can't afford them. They get very highly paid for what they do, and that's one of the sacrifices they have to make.'

Since the rents for photographic studios in London are very high, few photographers can afford to waste floor space on elaborate changing room facilities. If you're lucky, there'll be a small changing room with a mirror, but usually there'll be a small corner curtained or screened off for you to get changed in. Modelling is a business in which you can't afford to be shy, and anyway in one sense photographers are a bit like doctors – the female body is their livelihood, and they're far more interested in getting on with the work, than in anything else.

Once you've changed, you'll probably be asked to stand on a huge sheet of paper, suspended from the ceiling like a giant kitchen-roll and spread along the floor, to eliminate any detail in the background that might detract from the garment you're modelling. Since the paper is usually white and modern cameras pick up any little mark, you'll be expected to have covered the soles and heels of your shoes with masking tape before you arrive – naturally you won't have worn them on the way – so that they don't leave black marks on the paper.

You must also be very careful in the studio and watch where you're putting your feet – some photographers put their cameras on the floor, since it's the one place they can't fall from, and one careless step from you could do several hundred pounds' worth of damage. Watch out for the cables from the lights, too – not only could you do some expensive damage, you could also hurt yourself, and if you burnt your face, for instance, it would mean an end to your photographic modelling career.

But obviously a pretty face, good figure, the ability to keep your shoes clean and not fall over the equipment aren't by themselves going to make you into a top model. What sets a handful of girls above the rest is their ability to 'project', to come alive in front of a camera. The most beautiful girl in the world won't do a thing for the dress she's wearing or the product she's selling if she's dead from the neck up. Barry Lategan likens the ability to project to acting. 'It's not a question of pushing yourself all the time, it's more the ability to be exactly what's needed in every case. If you're modelling a lovely floaty chiffon dress, you've got to get across a soft, romantic floaty feeling, and if you're modelling swimwear on a beach, you've got to look as though the sun is beating down on your skin. It's largely an instinctive thing, though you obviously get better with experience. I'm not saying a girl ought to be dim, but if you get one who thinks too hard about what she's trying to do, the look is forced, it isn't natural.'

The photographer will tell you what he's after, perhaps play music to help you move naturally and gracefully, or put ideas into your head to create the mood he wants. As with your portfolio session, it's vitally important that you and the photographer can communicate if the shots are going to be a success. 'When I'm working,' says Shirley Anne, 'I don't even notice the camera at all. It's the man behind it I'm relating to. If I thought about it and realized I was leaping about and making faces at a *machine*, they'd have to come and take me away.'

On a session, the concept behind the pictures is the photographer's – or the fashion editor's or advertising executive's – but most of them welcome constructive ideas from the model. 'I think it's also very important for a girl to have an interest in clothes,' says Grace Coddington. 'It's so depressing when you give a girl something to put on and she clearly doesn't have a clue what the garment is all about. No matter how pretty she is, if the understanding isn't there, she looks wooden and hopeless.' Billie Figg agrees. 'One of my favourite models is very small, so I can only use her for tops and accessories, but I do use her whenever I can because she's so enthusiastic, always throws herself wholeheartedly into what we're trying to do, and it shows in the results.'

Naturally it's easy to be enthusiastic about a dress that really suits you, but a top model can make an old flour sack look stunning. 'It is harder to project nasty clothes,' says Shirley Anne. 'You look in the mirror and think

"I hate myself," and if that comes across in the picture, you'll never sell that dress to anyone.'

One of the criticisms you'll often hear levelled at you as a model is that you are becoming obsessed with yourself and the way you look, but that's inevitable in a way, since your looks are your livelihood, and, Billie Figg believes, desirable. 'Once a girl has done her face and her hair and is ready, there's got to be a degree of self-satisfaction with the finished result or else you just won't get the best out of her.'

On the other hand, girls who spend an eternity making themselves look as *they* want, irritate Niké Williams of *Honey* no end. 'I had three girls on a session the other day, and one of them took hours longer than the rest. When she finally appeared I had to say "I asked you to put eyeliner right round your eyes and you haven't, have you?" and then she started, "Well, my eyes are a bit close together and if I do that . . ." All day she kept niggling at me – why was one of the other girls doing all the solo shots and not her, and wouldn't I like to use her on the cover. She's a stunningly beautiful girl, but I doubt if I'll use her again and I wouldn't dream of taking her on a trip abroad. Can you imagine being stuck in a hotel somewhere for ten days with someone like that?'

Given the choice of two equally suitable girls, all the fashion editors pick the girl with the nicer disposition for any trips abroad. 'I won't take girls who aren't prepared to help,' says Grace Coddington, 'who just throw clothes on the floor when they've finished with them and expect me to pick them up. I'm not a ladies' maid and I don't like being treated as one!'

Sessions abroad are not paid holidays and since most trips are to the sun – in spite of that old chestnut, few people really want to show bikinis on Brighton Beach in January – you'll be starting work very early in the morning, when the light is good and the heat not too great, so if you've been out half the night, or have had a bit too much of the local vino or overdid the sunbathing the day before, you're not going to be at your best at 6 am. 'You need to be very sensible about looking after yourself,' says Grace Coddington, 'and very strong. If you've only got ten days to get the job done, you simply can't afford to have a girl falling ill.'

But even the most conscientious and professional model can't guarantee that she won't go down with appendicitis or a virus, and since very few foreign countries have any form of National Health Service, it's sensible to take out an insurance policy before you go. 'In Spain these days,' says Peter Noble, 'even a simple filling at the dentist's can cost around forty pounds, so a holiday insurance policy at ten pence a day is a very sound investment.'

Photographic modelling, then, is extremely hard work. Long hours, a lot of hanging about, and not knowing what time you'll be able to get away. You can say 'It's six o'clock and I'm only booked till six', but if the session isn't finished it means everyone coming back another day and costs a lot of money, so though you're within your rights that kind of behaviour won't win you friends or any future bookings from the people involved. If you're on location, conditions can be primitive and the work itself physically exhausting. Peter Noble recalls shooting an advertisement for a car in Cyprus. 'To show how roomy it is, we had a model getting out of it, and she got in and out of that car *seventy-eight* times! By the time we finished, it took a good hour and a half for the life to return to her thigh muscles.'

A really good photographic model needs not only the looks and the figure, she also needs the stamina, the enthusiasm and the right attitude to herself and her work. 'Most girls start their careers at seventeen, eighteen,' says Barry Lategan, 'which is about the most impressionable age, and if they're successful it's very hard for them to keep their feet on the ground – they're meeting interesting, glamorous people, and being invited to all kinds of exciting places, but a serious, working model can't afford to live that kind of life. She has to be in bed early most nights if she's got bookings next day or she won't be at her best.'

Grace Coddington, who's seen modelling from both sides of the fence, says, 'It can be a marvellous profession – the money's good, the people talented and interesting, you can travel, or take a few weeks off when you feel like it and it's not nine-to-five. As long as you're strong, mentally and physically, and you can keep your head, then I'd recommend it to any girl who wanted to give it a try.'

12 A day in the life of a photographic model

7.00 am The day starts for Josephine Florent, twenty-one-year-old, up-and-coming photographic model who is featured regularly in *Honey, 19, Cosmopolitan* and *Vogue*, in her parents' flat near Regent's Park, when her mother wakes her with a cup of tea. Twenty minutes later, having dropped off to sleep again, she gets up, washes and dresses, has another cup of tea and a glass of fresh orange juice – her version of breakfast. This morning she doesn't have to worry about putting her make-up on – at nine she's due at the studio of Christa Peters, one of the leading female photographers, to do a beauty session for *Cosmopolitan*. 'They're doing the Chinese look,' Josephine says, 'so they've got a make-up artist coming along to do it for me.'

She's due to fly to Paris in the evening for a session with *Marie-Claire* the following day – she's been booked on the 6.10 pm flight, and since her second session of the day doesn't finish till 5 pm she doesn't think she'll make it, but just in case her agency can't book her on a later flight, she packs a change of clothes and her passport in her model bag.

8.30 Josephine gets a taxi at the top of the road – 'I spend a fortune on taxis. I always mean to take the tube or a bus, but I never seem to manage it.' She arrives at Christa Peters' studio in Kensington five minutes early, to find Christa setting up her equipment and both the make-up artist, Anthony Clavet, and the hair stylist for the session, Christian O'Leary, both of whom she's worked with before, waiting for her.

9.00 Josephine settles herself in the dressing-room, in front of the large, well-lit mirror – one of the reasons she likes working with Christa is that her studio is so well equipped from a model's point of view – while Anthony goes through his vast selection of foundations to find the one that will turn her skin the 'old ivory' shade he wants. 'I've got another session this after-noon,' she says, laughing, 'so if you don't make me look too Chinese, the make-up will do for that, too.'

9.15   Christian comes in with two wigs for Josephine to try on. One, which she'd worn in another oriental session a few weeks earlier, had been cut short by mistake and though it makes her look like something Chairman Mao would have been proud of, it is, Christa decides, very unsexy. She prefers the other, longer wig. Josephine's relieved – she didn't think the first one did much for her, either.

9.30   Liz Smith, Fashion and Beauty Editor of *Cosmopolitan*, who has just arrived, agrees, so the longer wig it is. After a cup of coffee and a biscuit, Anthony begins to apply two slightly different shades of foundation to Josephine's face with a damp sponge. As he works, area by area, her face becomes visibly paler and more oriental-looking. As he applies Clinique's Everywhere Colour in yellow to her jaw and temples to give her whole face a faintly yellow tinge, they talk about mutual friends in the business, and trips they've both been on or are about to go on. It's all very relaxed and friendly.

9.45   He begins to work on her eyes. He's using no colour on the lids at all – it all goes underneath to alter the shape of the eye. In all he uses five different shadows – some cream, some powder – blending them all so carefully into one another that it's impossible to see, even close to, where one ends and another starts. It is a very slow process but because it's for a beauty shot, Josephine's make-up has got to be absolutely perfect.

10.25   To complete the eye make-up, Anthony wants a black line drawn inside her lower lashes, but because it is such a delicate operation, he asks her to do it herself. Liz Smith comes in and is delighted with the transformation – even without the wig on, Josephine is already looking remarkably oriental. 'I was a bit worried about that little spot on your chin,' Liz says, 'but it's completely invisible now.'

10.30   Christian appears to fit the wig. Josephine's own hair has to be hidden underneath it and because it's so long and thick, it has to be pinned up in neat pin-curls. 'Oh good,' she says, 'I need my hair curly for this afternoon's session.' The male model who is going to be in the photographs too has just arrived. 'What will he be wearing?' she asks, out of interest. 'Baby oil,' says the make-up man. Josephine's eyes widen. 'The agency said last night not to worry if there was a naked man in the picture, but I thought they were having me on!'

10.45   Christian starts to fit the wig. He uses heated tongs to make sure the hair hangs dead straight, then trims it to get it absolutely level. Since one hair fractionally longer than the others would show up in a photograph, that takes time, too.

11.15 It's Anthony's turn again – he brushes all the little bits of hair off Josephine's face – it's vital to remove every single one since the camera would probably pick it up – and retouches her make-up where necessary. Her hands will be in the shots, too, so he applies foundation to the backs of her fingers, and a warm, bright red nail varnish to her nails.

11.30 Liz and her assistant have been going through the clothes and jewellery they've brought along, to decide exactly which kimono, which rings, which bracelets, Josephine will wear. The atmosphere is still very amiable, but Christa is beginning to get a little impatient, since they are already an hour and a half behind schedule. Liz Smith briefs Josephine. 'We like a nice warm expression – not the sulky look some of the other magazines go for.' She, Crista and Anthony discuss what shape Josephine's lips should be. For the sake of authenticity, it ought to be an exaggerated red bow. Anthony duly paints in an exaggerated red bow, but Josephine's own very full lips show through underneath, so by mutual consent authenticity is sacrified on aesthetic grounds.

12.10 pm Josephine slips out of her own clothes into the red, patterned silk kimono that Liz has decided on, then joins the male model on the bamboo matting that has been laid out on the studio floor and draped over a framework to form a backdrop. Christa and Liz discuss the shape the photograph will eventually be on the page, and experiment with Josephine and the male model in different positions. They settle on the one they like – the two of them lying top to toe, propped up on their elbows, with Josephine resting her head on his knee. Christa arranges the various limbs precisely how she wants them. Liz makes sure the folds of the kimono are falling just right, and Christian gives her wig a final tug into place.

12.35 They're now ready to start, but first Christa takes a Polaroid to make sure that everything looks good on celluloid and that there are no flaws which may be invisible to the naked eye, but which would show up on a photograph. Twenty seconds later the picture is developed. 'Fantastic!' Christa says. Liz agrees, only she feels that Josephine ought to be shiny too. Anthony appears with a bottle of gleamer and applies it to her legs.

12.45 Christa settles down with her camera and begins to shoot. 'Look at me now, Josephine. Very sexy. Now, your head back . . . Great! Fantastic! Good girl. Bring your head over . . . Good, good! We're really getting it now . . .' Josephine really knows how to respond to the camera, moving slightly, changing her expression a fraction after every shot. 'It's not something I think about too much,' she says. 'It's instinctive. It has to be, really, otherwise it comes out looking forced.' Christa changes the film in her camera. 'Just imagine,' Christian says, 'your Mum's at home, making a cup of tea, without a clue about what you're doing here.' Everyone laughs.

1.00   As Christa and Liz discuss different poses, Josephine asks for some double-sided Sellotape to secure her kimono to her chest and stop it slipping.

1.05   Before Christa starts shooting again, Liz adjusts Josephine's bracelets, Christian runs a brush quickly over her wig and Anthony adds a bit more gleamer to her legs. More shots, more different positions and expressions. Another roll of film finished. Josephine shifts her weight gratefully off the elbow she's been leaning on, and rubs her arm to get rid of the bamboo matting imprints on her skin.

1.20   Yet another position – this time Josephine is lying on her stomach with her face against the male model's chest. Yet more adjustments to kimono, jewellery, wig and make-up – when you're dealing with perfectionists, every single detail has to be absolutely right. Christa settles down again with her camera. 'Wonderful,' she says clicking away, as Josephine responds. 'Fantastic! Good, girl, Josephine. Okay, that's it! Finish!' Faint cheers go up all round.

1.45   Josephine slips out of her kimono and into her wrap while Christian takes off her wig and brushes her own hair out into a mass of curls. She dresses rapidly in the loo – suddenly the dressing-room is full of people – gets Christa's assistant to sign her book, saying how many hours she's worked that morning, then packs her things into her model bag and says good-bye to everyone.

2.00   She hails a taxi in Kensington High Street to take her to her next appointment at the studio of Tony Boase, just behind Bond Street. She's due there at 2.30, so there'll be no time for lunch. If she's lucky, someone might be able to slip out and get her a cup of coffee and a sandwich.

2.25   She arrives at the studio to find her airline ticket to Paris waiting for her, and June Marsh from *Woman's Own* fashion department sorting out the clothes for the afternoon's session. The other model, Anna Bjorn, who's been working all morning, is taking a few minutes' well-earned rest.

2.30   Josephine borrows a couple of Anna's heated rollers to curl her fringe – she has some tongs in her model bag, but since Anna's rollers are already plugged in and hot, there isn't much point in heating up her tongs. In about five seconds, she wipes off the eyeshadow that had taken Anthony forty-five minutes to put on. Quickly she applies more eyeshadow, more convention-ally this time, and some blusher to counteract the paleness of her foundation. While she works, she tries to eat the cucumber sandwich someone has bought her, and drink a cup of scalding hot coffee.

2.45   June Marsh hands her the first outfit – a skirt, sweater and jacket in green and cream, and biscuit-coloured shoes, so Josephine pulls out a pair of pale matching tights from her model bag and puts them on.

3.00   Tony Boase, June and Josephine go out into the mews to shoot this outfit. The sun is very bright and very hot, and the stiff breeze blows Josephine's hair everywhere but it still looks good. Tony asks her to stand in front of someone's door and pretend she's ringing the bell. 'Don't actually ring it, though,' he says. 'I know the woman who lives there!' As Tony starts to shoot, Josephine buttons and unbuttons the jacket, slips one hand in and out of the pocket, puts one foot on the doorstep, takes it off again. The sun is in her eyes, so she finds it impossible to look naturally at the camera, but for once it doesn't matter – it's a reshoot of a session done earlier with another model, so they don't want to see her face.

3.20   Back inside. While June organizes Josephine's next outfit, she rings her agency to see if they can change the booking to Paris for a later flight. They say they'll see what they can do and call her back. She puts on the first outfit of the session – autumn clothes in shades of red to be shot against a red background – and steps up on to the low platform at the far end of the studio. Tony Boase takes a Polaroid which both he and June check for any little defects, and since there are none, he begins to shoot. For the first few shots, Josephine is a little bit stiff – she has never worked with Tony before and so isn't quite sure what he wants from her – but she soon gets into it. 'That's it. Now sway a bit, get some movement into the coat. That's nice, really nice. Now throw your head back and laugh.' Josephine puts her hand up to her hair as she does as she's asked. 'Oh, love it, love it!' says Tony.
    It's very hot in the studio what with the sun outside and the photographic lighting, and, of course, the clothes are thick winter clothes, so as soon as

Tony has finished shooting the first outfit, Josephine gratefully dives for the can of ice-cold Coca Cola that Tony has produced from the fridge, and the cooling electric fan in the corner.

4.00   Josephine's agency rings back and say that they've managed to book her on the 8.00 pm flight to Paris instead, at which she is greatly relieved.

5.20   Four more outfits and five rolls of film later, the session is over. Josephine asks Tony's assistant to book her a cab as she gets out of the final outfit and into her own clothes, gets her book signed and says good-bye to everyone.

5.45   She gets home, asks the cab to come back for her in half an hour, and sets about getting herself organized for the Paris trip. She packed the essentials this morning in case she did have to try and make the 6.10 pm flight after all, so now just checks that she's got everything, says good-bye to her parents and goes out to meet the cab.

7.00   She arrives at Heathrow, checks in, and slumps gratefully on to a chair in the departure lounge.

8.00   The plane takes off on time, and once they're airborne Josephine falls asleep. An hour later she's at Orly airport, outside Paris. She clears customs very quickly, since she's carrying all her luggage with her – her handbag and her model bag – then gets a taxi to the Elysée Palace Hotel where she's staying.

10.15   She checks in, goes up to her room and rings a couple of friends who are also working in Paris, but they're out – it's 14 July, Bastille Day, and everybody's celebrating. 'Just as well,' she says, 'I've got to be up at six o'clock to get my hair washed ready for the session at nine.' Instead of a night out, she has a bath, watches the firework display in the city from her balcony for a while, then goes to bed.

11.00   Josephine's fast asleep.

13 Male modelling

For many years, male modelling was placed in the same category in most people's minds as ballet dancing and flower arranging – something that only attracted homosexuals and certainly not the sort of career any sensible man would dream of taking seriously – but in the last decade or so, as people have begun to realize that it can be an extremely rewarding, interesting way of life, that stigma has begun to fade.

Although there isn't anything like as much work for men as there is for girls – even the mail order catalogues, one of the most lucrative sources of work, use about one man for every two or three girls – a male model's career can last a good deal longer, perhaps as long as thirty years. For one thing, a lot of the work for men is character work – just think of all the adverts you see which feature milkmen, bank managers, doctors, grandfathers, city gents – where a few grey hairs and wrinkles are certainly no handicap. And for another, in fashion and general photographic work, maturity is a real asset. Look at any glossy magazine – the man escorting the girl in the beautiful evening dress probably looks around thirty, sophisticated and mature, not a fresh-faced boy next door.

'The ideal look for male models at the moment,' says Neville Gates who runs Nevs, one of the most successful male agencies, 'is around thirty. That doesn't mean that the model has to be thirty – a couple of my busiest models are twenty-six and forty-two respectively, but they both *look* around thirty. If an eighteen-year-old who looks his age comes to see me, I tell him to go away and come back in ten years.'

Fashion photographer Francis Loney agrees. 'The face has got to go with the clothes to some extent. It's silly to show an expensive, elegant suit on a nineteen-year-old boy, because the people who are likely to buy that suit are going to be a good bit older than that, and they do need to identify, to some extent, with the model.'

Gil Barber, a successful male model who runs the male side of Gavin Robinson's agency, is wary of laying down rules. 'I was told years ago that

I'd never make it as a model, so if somebody really wanted to do it, then I'd tell them to have a go. Besides, I don't think you ever know which faces are going to sell. Could be that a young, fresh-faced kid will turn out to be *the* face of '76, but I suppose if you want to work steadily and unspectacularly over a number of years, then the mature look is probably best.'

Of course there is work for the younger man – in the younger-style sections of catalogues, for instance, and in some adverts aimed mainly at teenagers – but probably not enough to make a living.

With girls, it's impossible to pin down potential employers such as photographers and fashion editors as to the qualities they look for, but most of them seem to have a clearer idea about what they're looking for in men. Geoffrey Aquilina Ross, who's responsible for men's fashion in the London *Evening Standard*, looks for strong, interesting faces rather than pretty ones. 'Pretty faces don't relate to real people and real events somehow, and when you're presenting clothes to people, you're trying to show them on a man who is everyone's secret ideal – the sort of man most people can look at and think "Oh, yes, he's a bit like me, or my husband or my son."' Francis Loney also prefers strong, 'lived-in' faces to smooth, pretty ones, and not only on aesthetic grounds. 'I often find that people who are very beautiful are much more difficult to work with because they've always relied simply on their beauty to carry them through, so they're inclined to be lazy.'

In spite of the popular myth, effeminate-looking men do not get much work. 'Effeminacy just doesn't sell clothes,' says Diana Knab who runs her husband's photographic studio and has a large say in the selection of male models for advertising and catalogue work, 'and the best models from our point of view are the meaty-looking, very masculine ones. It's surprisingly difficult to tell just from looking at a man whether this quality will come across in a photograph – an astonishing number of the big, lumpy men look very miminy-piminy through a camera.'

As with the girls, there are basic physical requirements. For fashion work, you should be at least 5′ 10″, though if you're more than 6′ 2″ you'll find that few manufacturers' standard ranges will fit you. For advertising work, you could be as tall as 6′ 4″, but if you're taller than that your chances of getting work, apart from the odd 'freak' job, are fairly remote. For photographic work height isn't quite so critical, though if you're much under 5′ 9″ the amount of work available will be limited – you couldn't really appear with female models, for instance, since most of them are 5′ 7″ or more, and with high-heeled shoes on, they'd tower over you.

Ideally, your body should be well proportioned, with an inside leg measurement of at least 32″ and a 38″ to 40″ chest, and your build average. Mr Universe muscles are as much of a disadvantage as a pot belly, since your main function is to look so good in the clothes you're modelling that your audience wants to buy them, and if there are bulges everywhere, whether they are muscles or fat, you won't sell clothes.

Whether you're planning to concentrate on fashion shows or photographic work, it's vital to know how to use your body, how to move well, and before you do anything else, you must learn how to walk properly. For girls, the model walk is a whole new skill and one they wouldn't use any-where but on the catwalk or in a showroom, but what you'll be learning is how to walk as you ought to be walking all the time. 'Most men walk appallingly badly these days,' says Jon Sutton, a male model who now also lectures on the subject, 'head down, shoulders rounded, shuffling along! It creates a terribly bad impression.'

The first thing to learn is how to stand properly. Starting at the top – head up so that you're looking straight in front of you and not down your nose, shoulders back and level, diaphragm pulled in tight and your bottom tucked in. If you have been standing badly all your life, of course it will feel strange at first, but that doesn't mean it's unnatural. You must practise all the time – when you're queuing for a bus or for a drink at lunch-time – until it becomes second nature and you'll be able to relax as easily in that position as you used to slouching up against a wall.

When you start to walk, remember always to lead off with your front foot, and to keep the weight on the balls of your feet. Don't put your weight on your heels – not only will it make you sound like a regiment of soldiers, it will also make you look flat-footed, whereas walking on the balls of your feet puts a spring in your step which always looks very masculine. You can swing your arms a little as you walk but do make sure you don't look too military. Always keep your head up – nothing makes you look less confident than constantly watching your feet. And don't be afraid to look at your audience and smile. Remember that the majority of your audiences will be female, so they'll already be on your side.

There are no special modelling turns for men – the keynote is naturalness and you should turn as simply and as neatly as you can, pivoting on the balls of your feet, though, not turning on your heels. 'The moment a man starts doing elaborate turns or starts putting his hands on his hips or fiddling with the clothes he's modelling, he starts to look effeminate,' Jon Sutton believes, 'and that's fatal as far as selling the garments he's modelling goes. Everything should be kept as unfussy and as natural looking as possible.'

Obviously, the style of modelling depends very much on the clothes you're wearing. If you're showing a very formal City suit, then you model it crisply, with an air of authority, but if it's a sports jacket and slacks, then you could more or less stroll along the catwalk in a very relaxed fashion.

When you're modelling a suit or a jacket, then you should start out with the middle button only done up. Once you're on the catwalk, you can unbutton it without looking down by sliding one hand under the flap of the jacket, keeping your thumb on top, and pushing the button through the button hole, to show the audience how the garment looks both done up and undone. If the suit has a waistcoat or a particularly attractive lining, then take hold of the jacket just above the top button, with your thumbs under the lapels, and hold it open just long enough for your audience to see what's underneath.

It's very rare these days to find a man modelling alone – he'll either be with a girl or group of girls or other men – so it's important to get used to working with other people, which involves a lot of discipline and a good sense of timing, particularly now that most the big shows are staged like musicals.

When it comes to looking after your assets – your looks and your health – many of the rules that apply to the girls apply to you too – those concerning diet and exercise, for example, and hair and skin care. Your skin is just as important to you professionally as a girl's is, if not more so – don't forget that you can't work the same miracles with make-up to camouflage a spot that appears on the morning of a big session, so prevention is infinitely better than cure. If you do suffer from acne, and young men often do seem to get it more acutely than girls of the same age, then your best bet is to consult your doctor and ask him to refer you to a skin specialist. Although diet isn't the root cause of acne, it can play a part in controlling it to some degree, so if you do suffer from spots, then try cutting out fried and highly spiced foods for a while, and eat as much fresh fruit – citrus fruit in particular – and vegetables as you can. If you suffer from razor rash, perhaps your after-shave lotion is too strong and the alcohol content is irritating your skin, so stop using it and see if the problem clears up. If it doesn't, then, again, try consulting your doctor.

Make-up isn't a subject that need concern you, although if you have a fairly dark five o'clock shadow some photographers may want you to use a little pancake to help cover it up. If you're working under very strong lights which drain all the colour from your face, then you could use a little bronzer – most men's toiletries manufacturers make one – or Leichner's Cream Cake, a product created for television announcers who needed a bit of colour but didn't want to look made-up when they were out and about between announcements. Avoid those fake tanning creams – they are difficult to apply evenly, and they tend to turn your skin a rather unflattering orangey-brown. A sun-ray lamp is probably the best of all, if you can afford one. Not only will it give you a light tan – provided, of course, you use it carefully and don't wind up lobster red – it will also help to clear up any spots that you may have.

Beards and moustaches are not a good idea when you're modelling because they do limit you. If you go to an audition with a moustache and they're looking for someone clean-shaven, they will automatically reject you, and even if you say you're willing to shave it off, they might not be able to picture you without it and still turn you down. Also, it's worth remembering that if your index cards show you with a moustache and then you shave it off, you must have a new set done, which will be expensive.

Although hair fashions change with the times, hair shouldn't be too long – just reaching your collar at the back is about right. Shoulder-length locks may look all right with jeans, but they don't really go with a formal three-piece suit. A lightly tousled look is fashionable, but that's not to say you should look as though you've just crawled out of bed. Make sure your hair is cut regularly by a good hairdresser, and that it is always clean – there are few things more off-putting than lank, greasy hair.

The same is true of body odour. Although personal freshness is of the utmost importance to any model, you need to be extra-specially careful about it because men do perspire more heavily than girls. A daily bath or shower, along with clean underwear, socks and shirt, is a 'must' and always use an effective deodorant and anti-perspirant. Apart from the fact that it is extremely unpleasant for your colleagues if you do have a problem with body odour, remember that much of the time you'll be wearing clothes that aren't your own, and no manufacturer is going to be very pleased if the garments come back smelling and with perspiration stains under the arms.

If you like using an after-shave or cologne, then choose one that doesn't irritate your skin and isn't too powerful, and try to match your talc and deodorant, too, so that you don't wind up smelling like a men's gift department at Christmas time. In most fashion shows, the clothes will be provided for you, but for a lot of photographic work, non-fashion advertising in particular, you will be expected to provide your own. Remember that it isn't the *size* of your wardrobe that matters – if you have a few good-quality, versatile basics that fit you perfectly and are always in immaculate condition, plus a good selection of shirts and ties which, of course, all go with your suit, jackets and trousers, you won't go far wrong.

To start at the bottom, you'll need two pairs of shoes, one black, one brown, in a simple classic style – no wedges or large platforms, for instance – which you keep cleaned and in a good state of repair. You should have at least two pairs of trousers, one in a dark colour such as black, navy or chocolate brown, and one in a paler colour, such as pale grey or beige, and again the style should be fairly classic because it won't date so quickly. 'I

think male models should aim at being, not old-fashioned, but a little *con-
servative* in their clothes,' Jon Sutton believes. 'Obviously you should watch
the trends, but don't go the whole hog. For one thing, high fashion dates
so fast and for another, you want people to remember *you*, not what you
were wearing.'

A pair of jeans – faded by all means, but not falling apart – is always useful
and, if you can afford it, a pair of sporty trousers, check or tweed, would
come in handy too. You should have at least one V-necked and one polo-
necked sweater in a versatile colour such as black or grey, and as many cotton
shirts, both patterned and plain, as you can manage. It's a good idea to have
a couple of plain white shirts, so that one of them is *always* washed, pressed
and ready to wear, since you'll often find that you'll be asked to take a white
shirt along to a session. A good selection of ties, again both plain and
patterned, is essential, and remember to watch the fashion trends. If your
tie is exactly the right width for now, and the knot is the right size, then you
will look extremely fashionable even if your suit is two or three years old.
At the moment scarves are fashionable, so a selection of those – perhaps a
sporty knitted one, or one of those tartan woollen ones that French boys
wear so effectively, plus a silk one and a couple of cotton squares for tying
round your neck, cowboy-style, would be worth having too.

You must have at least one suit, and if you can only afford one when
you're starting out, make sure that it fits you perfectly – that the trousers and
sleeves, for instance, are the right length – and that it's a fairly formal style
in a dark colour, navy or charcoal grey, for example, that will serve a multitude of purposes. A sports jacket or a blazer is also very useful, though these
days, if your budget is limited, you might find that a velvet jacket or even
a suit, which can look very casual with an open-necked shirt or polo-necked
sweater or, with an evening shirt and velvet bow-tie, can double up as
evening wear, is a better investment. When you're starting out, a dinner
jacket isn't essential – they are very expensive and they do date fairly quickly,
too.

Like the girls, you'll need some kind of model bag, although it won't be
anything like as heavy as theirs are. You should always carry two pairs of
shoes, a couple of extra shirts and ties, a change of socks, handkerchiefs or
tissues, and it's a good idea to carry a wet pack, with soap, flannel, deodorant,
and a towel. You'll almost always be told what's wanted in the way of
clothes before you go to a job, so you don't need to carry a vast selection
around with you. It's not a good idea to travel in the clothes you've been
asked to wear for a session. For one thing, they'll get very creased, and for
another that child sitting next to you on the bus may well drop his ice-cream
in your lap. Don't use a suitcase to carry your gear, though – use a grip for

the smaller items and one of those soft polythene zip-up covers for your suit or jacket and trousers.

Once you have collected together the right clothes and accessories, don't be tempted to think that all you have to do is put them on, and hey presto! you're a great male model. You must learn to 'feel' clothes, to understand what they're doing for you, and know how to show them off to advantage. Geoffrey Aquilina Ross of the *Evening Standard* is still surprised by the number of reasonably successful male models who still haven't acquired those skills. 'At the moment, it isn't the done thing among male models to show any real interest in clothes, and I don't really mind them turning up for a session looking scruffy, but I do find it irritating when I give them clothes to put on, and wind up dressing them myself because they don't know how to make the clothes look good. Basically, too many of them lack style.'

Once you've learnt to make the best of yourself, and have got together the tools of your trade, the next step is to find yourself a good agent. Most of the big model agencies have a male section, while others, Nevs for example, concentrate chiefly on men. What Neville Gates looks for in potential models, apart from saleable looks, is: 'No temperament, strict punctuality, complete unselfishness – I want them to consider me, the studio and the client, not merely themselves – and a sense of humour. Unfortunately, I have yet to find anyone with all those qualities.'

Gil Barber bewails the current lack of professionalism among the majority of male models. 'The guys who are working all the time are the ones who've been in the business for five, ten, even fifteen years. Most of the new ones have got the idea that modelling is some kind of highly paid game, and they just aren't prepared to spend the time and energy to get a decent wardrobe together or to work at their trade. There are exceptions though, like the guy who came to us a while back, who seemed wrong in every way. Then he decided to get his hair cut like Robert Redford in *The Way We Were* and suddenly he looked just like Redford, so he began to work on that image, got the right clothes together, practised facial expressions, the whole bit, and now he's one of the busiest models in Europe. Sadly, very few guys are prepared to put that kind of effort into their careers.'

In general men seem to take longer to establish themselves than girls – Gil Barber reckons it's usually about two years before a man is working regularly enough to make his living from modelling – and so in most cases you'd be advised to find a part-time job to help you pay the rent at first. A lot of models take evening jobs in pubs or restaurants so that they are free for interviews and bookings during the day. Others combine modelling with acting, but Neville Gates doesn't think it's a very good idea. 'I won't take on actor-models because they are two separate careers that you can't easily combine. I mean, at the moment, I'm booking models for fashion shows next spring, which will involve them in having the clothes fitted on them in a few weeks' time. Now supposing one of the models is also an actor and between the fittings and the show a good part comes up – he's going to take it, which leaves the client with clothes that don't fit anyone else perfectly, and of course, it doesn't do my reputation any good.'

Francis Loney isn't keen on actor-models in general, from a photographic point of view though, naturally, there are exceptions. 'A good male model has the ability to react to a given situation and to know exactly what expression and gestures are right, which *isn't* an acting skill. Actors usually exaggerate everything – they're used to projecting to a big audience that's miles away – and ruin the subtlety of the shot.'

You will find that there is a lot of opportunity for foreign travel – most catalogues are shot out of season in locations like the Canary Islands, Greece, North Africa – and the rules that apply to the girls about trips abroad apply equally to you. Remember that you are there to work, not primarily to have fun, and that if anything happens to you that prevents you working, you're not only wasting everybody else's time, you are costing your employers a fortune. One up-and-coming young model was booked for a fortnight's catalogue work in Tangier. On the third day, he hired a motorbike without telling anyone, had an accident which meant his left arm had to be heavily bandaged, and so would no longer fit into any of the jackets he was to model. All the photographs of him had to be taken with his left arm out of shot, which created enormous problems for the photographer and the client. 'Needless to say,' says Gil Barber, 'he will never work for that firm again. In this business, there are no second chances.'

The way to ensure regular bookings year after year is not only to be thoroughly professional – no coming down to breakfast unshaven for instance – but also to be as pleasant to work with as you can. 'If you're working with someone for just a couple of hours,' says Francis Loney, 'then the working relationship isn't too important, but if you're going to be working together for a couple of days, or even weeks, then it is critical. I have to like the models I'm working with if I'm going to do my best work, and though of course I do make an effort, I expect them to make an effort too. It may seem hard, but I think that creating a good creative atmosphere is largely the model's responsibility. The moment you get somebody who starts being temperamental, that's it – I get uptight, the client gets uptight and the results inevitably suffer.'

Diana Knab, whose job involves looking after models all the time, finds the men more difficult to cope with than the girls. 'I suppose it's partly because you expect fully grown men to be able to look after themselves. Girls are generally much more amenable – I can just say to them "Change of plan – we're doing this now", and it's okay, but with the men there's always an inquisition – "Oh, why? Can't we have a coffee break now?" – and they have to be persuaded and buttered up.'

Gil Barber, on the other hand, believes that the men who are making a career of modelling are much easier to cope with than the girls. 'If a man is married, then I find he will listen to what I have to say and is willing to do whatever is asked of him without a murmur because he has responsibilities, a family perhaps and a mortgage, and he is simply interested in earning a living.'

And it can be a very good living if you have the right physical requirements and, more important, the right attitude – treat the business seriously and be prepared to work very hard. 'It's a marvellous business,' Gil Barber believes, 'you can travel, you can get an education if you make the most of the opportunities that come along, you can have a lot of fun, and you're also extremely lucky in that you can make money – and a lot of money, too – doing something you enjoy.'

14   A day in the life of a male model

For David Warbeck, thirty-two-year-old actor-model, the day always starts reasonably early. For one thing, he likes to have plenty of time to get himself ready for the day, and for another, with a four-year-old daughter in the house there isn't the chance to sleep late. His call this morning is for eleven so he doesn't have to get up too early.

7.30 am   He gets up, makes a cup of tea, then has a shower and washes his hair. He shaves very thoroughly – he has a fairly heavy beard so if he doesn't he's inclined to get his five o'clock shadow around lunch-time. Normally he doesn't bother with breakfast at all – often there isn't time, since his wife Lois works too, and one of them has to get Lucy, their daughter, off to school – but this morning he has a boiled egg. 'We're working on location today, and you never know when you'll get the chance to eat again.'

The location today is Hyde Park – not quite as glamorous as some of the places he's been working in lately, like Tokyo, and Rhodes. 'It sounds great, but in Rhodes we were doing a winter catalogue and modelling sheepskin coats in ninety-five degrees in the shade just isn't funny.'

He'll be modelling a knitwear company's spring range of shirts and sweaters, so he won't need to take any of his own, only a couple of pairs of trousers, one in dark brown gaberdine, the other in beige linen, and a pair of brown shoes that will go with both. In the years that he's been modelling, David has built up a 'rather luxurious work wardrobe' which he almost never wears off-duty. 'You'll find a lot of male models tend to live in jeans and T-shirts, because they get so fed up with having to look elegant and formal on duty.'

Into the big Majorcan straw basket that he uses as his model bag, he puts a sponge bag, some make-up – a stick of theatrical pancake to mask his beard, and a tube of bronzer to give him a little extra colour, a box of cigars – 'I don't smoke but I find they're a very useful prop', a mirror, brush and comb, and his diary and accounts book. Today, as it's midsummer and comparatively warm, he doesn't bother with his 'survival kit' – a couple of flasks of hot tea, which have saved his life on a number of occasions. 'I found that I usually wound up catering for everybody else too, so I tend to keep a bit quiet about it these days.'

10.25   He puts his model bag and the two pairs of trousers, which he checked last night, put on a hanger and covered with a polythene bag, into his brown Mini and sets off for Hyde Park.

10.50   Arrives in the Serpentine car park to find the wardrobe van – which also serves as a mobile changing-room – already there, and the two female models inside putting on their make-up. 'I always think we have a much easier time than the girls,' David says, 'because we don't have to bother about all that. If the call is for eleven, they need to be here about quarter past ten to get their hair done and their faces made-up, while I can just turn up ten minutes before we start and be ready to go almost at once.'

11.00   Jeannie Fraser-Allen, the public relations co-ordinator for the knit-wear firm, hands David the shirt and sweater he'll be modelling first, and he goes off to change at the back of the van. Once he's dressed, he runs a comb through his hair, then roughs it up slightly with his fingers. He checks his face in his small magnifying mirror and settles for just a touch of bronzer at this stage, then opens a small metal box, takes out the tiny piece of plastic inside, slips it between his two front teeth and instantly the small gap he had disappears. 'The gap between my teeth is fine for everyday, but it does show up rather badly on photographs, so rather than have two perfectly good teeth crowned, I got my dentist to make me this little plastic fill-in for photographic work. It's really very good indeed – I've done toothpaste commercials in it, and even in feature films, with my face about ten foot high on the screen, you still can't detect it.'

11.15   The van drives over to the other side of the Serpentine, and while Jeannie and Francis Loney, the photographer, walk on ahead to sort out a boat for them to be photographed in, at the boat hire jetty, David and Philo, one of the female models, walk on behind. As they walk, they discuss the problems of finding a really good agent – or rather Philo talks and David listens. They have both had their fair share of problems in the past but are both now very happy with their agencies. Bobton's in Philo's case, Askew's in David's. 'They are very understanding about the acting side of my career and do everything they can to help me keep the two things going. Other agencies I've been with didn't like the fact that I acted too, so it was best for us to part company.'

11.40   They arrive at the jetty to find that Jeannie has already organized a rowing boat, which is tied up alongside, for them to sit in. Jeannie hands David an apple. 'It's a prop,' she warns, 'so don't eat it yet.' 'The number of apples I've had almost to my lips . . .' David rolls his eyes.

11.50   David and Philo get themselves settled in the boat, looking like the happy young couple they're supposed to be. Francis gets ready to take a Polaroid to check that the shot is what Jeannie wants. The sun is in and out every few seconds, which doesn't make the job any easier.

12.00 noon   Jeannie makes a few final adjustments to David's sweater to show off the slightly puffed sleeves to advantage, then Francis begins to shoot. 'Look as though you're really enjoying yourselves! That's it! Divine, divine!'

12.10 pm   The two rolls of 'double' shots completed, Philo gets out of the boat, nearly managing to tip David into the water. 'Right now,' Francis says, 'let's have lots of action.' David picks up an oar and starts to wave it about. 'I feel like a galley slave,' he says, laughing. Jeannie decides she'd like him in a more reflective mood now, so he decides to light up one of his 'prop' cigars. Unfortunately nobody has any matches, so they have to beg a light from one of the boys who work on the boats.

12.20   Francis then takes two rolls of 'single' shots and once he's finished David goes back to the van to change. The assistant is waiting with hot coffee, which David drinks while he's changing into the dark brown trousers that go with the next sweater he has to model. Jeannie arrives back at the van – unfortunately Francis suspects there's something wrong with the camera he used for the black and white shots, so just to be on the safe side he wants to shoot them again. Could David change back into the first outfit, then, and be back at the jetty as quickly as possible?

12.45   Back to the jetty for the retakes!

1.25   When David, Jeannie and Francis get back to the van, they find there is a slight problem with the law. Under a new regulation, the permit which all photographers need for shooting in public places doesn't cover Royal Parks such as Hyde Park, so after rapid consultations they decide to move on to non-Royal Holland Park. There's no point in David leaving his car at the Serpentine, so he picks it up from the car park and follows the van.

1.45   The convoy arrives in Holland Park and David changes into the next outfit. He quickly checks his face in the mirror – his beard is beginning to show a little, so he smooths on some pancake and a little more bronzer, runs a comb through his hair and he's ready to go.

2.00   David, Philo and Bettan, the other model, make their way with Jeannie and Francis through the gardens to a quiet corner, with a bench up against an old, mellow brick wall. David settles himself on the bench, this time with Bettan, and looks just as relaxed and affectionate as he had with Philo. All part of the job. Jeannie spends a few minutes adjusting both their sweaters to make sure they look their best, while Francis gets ready to take the Polaroid. Both he and Jeannie are pleased with the result, so he begins to shoot for real. David and Bettan have often worked together before and so they're laughing and joking and teasing each other, which gives Francis exactly the kind of pictures he's after.

2.10   A park keeper appears, spiking litter – everyone notices him and pretends that they haven't. He doesn't say anything, though, just spikes a few ice-cream wrappers and wanders on past, much to everyone's relief.

2.20   A change of position – Jeannie wants Bettan and David standing in front of an old stone niche with ivy trailing over it, and chatting. A gang of kids, about ten or eleven, appear to watch, and jeer. 'Go on then, mister, give her a kiss then!' David doesn't turn a hair. 'A common occurrence,' he says with a grin, 'only usually there are twenty of them.' He stopped noticing the crowd that inevitably gathers round a location shoot a long time ago, and the 'nudge-nudge-wink-wink' grins of some of the men no longer bother him. 'People still assume that male models have got to be either homo-sexuals or idiots because there's still something not quite right about men "flaunting" themselves, but it doesn't worry me at all. I earn a very good living, I see the world at other people's expense, and I enjoy what I'm doing, so why should I worry?' He tends to find, though, that there is still a degree of snobbery about the profession socially – 'I've actually had people at dinner parties turn away and refuse to speak to me again when they find out what I do. So these days, if anyone asks, I usually say I'm a hooker!'

3.00   All the shots of David are finished – the girls are going on to another location in a hotel, but there aren't any more garments for David to show, so he goes back to the van to change into his own clothes. Jeannie has organized a picnic lunch – sandwiches, hot coffee and fresh fruit – so David slips the little plastic filler from between his front teeth and has a sandwich while he's waiting for Jeannie to sign his book.

3.30   He packs his things, says good-bye to everyone and leaves. His next stop is his agent's office in Victoria to discuss a possible booking in Milan the following week, but on the way he stops to ring his theatrical agent to find out if there is any news about the big film part he's up for. 'It's a little tricky at the moment, because the film people said they'd probably want to see me today or tomorrow, and of course I want to keep myself free for that, but on the other hand, I've got the chance of an extremely lucrative week's work in Milan next week, for which I'll have to fly out on Sunday. So if I don't hear from the film people before the week-end, I'm not sure what I'll do.' He spends half an hour talking it over with his agent, who's prepared to wait till the last minute for David to make his decision.

5.00   He leaves and heads for Holborn to see his accountant about his tax returns for last year, spends about twenty minutes with him, and gets home about half past six. It hasn't been a very tiring day, but since he's working again in the morning and it's an early start, he's planning to spend a quiet evening at home. After supper with his wife and daughter, he presses the shirts he's been asked to take on tomorrow's session – 'I don't see any reason why I shouldn't do it myself. After all, it is to do with my career, and since Lois has a career of her own, I wouldn't dream of asking her to do it' – checks that his suit is in immaculate shape and packs his bag ready for the morning.

11.00   He's in bed and asleep.

15 Teenagers, over-thirties and outsize ladies

Say 'model girl' to most people and the picture they immediately conjure up in their minds is of an elegant, sylph-like creature in her early twenties. Admittedly, the majority of models do fall into that category, but they by no means have a monopoly on the modelling business – just glance through the magazines on the bookstalls or through any big mail order company's catalogue, and you'll see girls who are younger, women who are a good deal older and a good deal bigger than the usual, youthful size 10. Obviously there is less work for specialist models than there is for the 'skinny' all-rounders, but on the other hand there are far fewer of them around, so there is far less competition and the demand for good teenage or older or outsize models is constant.

A 'teenage' model isn't simply a girl under twenty – some girls, like Twiggy, are top models at seventeen without ever having been teenage models, while others still qualify for that label at twenty-one or twenty-two. It's much more to do with a look – fresh, natural, bouncy – than with years. Good teenage models are few and far between because, apart from anything else, their careers are by their very nature strictly limited. Even the rare girl who still looks fifteen when she's twenty or twenty-one only has a working life in that market of five or six years, and for the majority of girls two or three years is about average. There is no lower age limit for launching yourself on a modelling career – you can start as soon as a magazine or catalogue company decides it wants to use you. Even if you're under sixteen, there is no legal limit on the amount of photographic modelling you can do, although most employers do play the game and arrange sessions after school hours, at week-ends or in the holidays. Television commercials, on the other hand, are controlled by the Child Performances Act, which limits the number of hours that anyone under sixteen can work, and your would-be employer would need a licence from the local authority before he could use you.

Almost all the rules that apply to models in general, also apply to you.

You should know how to walk well – admittedly there is very little live fashion work for teenagers, but it will be extremely useful if you decide to continue with your career once your teenage days are over, and learning good co-ordination will help you to move well and fluently in front of a camera. You should also know how to look after your assets and how to make the best of yourself.

It's worth paying extra-special attention to your skin, for instance, since you're at the age when teenage acne could be a problem, and even if you don't suffer from spots, it's never too early to start looking after your skin, making sure that you cleanse it properly every night without fail before you go to bed, and lightly moisturizing it every day.

Skill with make-up is something you must acquire, though at this stage you should use it only to camouflage less-than-perfect features or a problem skin, and to bring out your natural beauty. Ideally you ought to look as though you aren't wearing any make-up at all.

'When we book girls for sessions,' says Carolyn Woodward of the *Mirabelle* beauty room, 'we always specify that we want as little make-up as possible, and if the girl can take it, then no make-up at all. What we are always looking for is a young, fresh, natural look, and masses of thick make-up just doesn't go with that at all.' What Carolyn looks for in a model is a pretty, girl-next-door look, a slightly idealized version of the magazine's readers. 'We like good features – a smallish nose, nice white, even teeth and a big bright smile. The magazine's image is bright and bouncy and we want our models to look that way too. If a girl is very pretty in a sulky sort of way or obviously isn't lively and full of energy, then she wouldn't be right for us.'

As far as size is concerned, both Carolyn and Sue James, fashion and beauty editor of *Fab 208*, go for girls with a size 10 figure who are about 5′ 6″. 'We do use quite a few girls who are only 5′ 2″ or 3″,' says Sue James, 'because quite a few of our readers at fourteen or fifteen are only about that height, and quite a lot of teenage fashion is geared to that height.' *Mirabelle* will use the smaller girls for any fashion feature if their face and personality is right – as long as they use them by themselves, not with a group of taller girls, or on a bicycle or a horse, as then their lack of inches just doesn't show. All models need good agents, but in your case, because you are so young, it's even more important to find someone who will protect your interests and not allow you to be exploited. If you are sixteen, have left school, and are starting out on a full-time modelling career, then your best bet is to try all the good general model agencies – not only will they help you to get established, but, because they are handling ordinary models too, they will be able to help you make the often difficult transition from the teenage market to the adult one, when the time comes. If you are under sixteen and still at school, then you might be better off with an agency that specializes in children and young teenagers, because they are used to coping with the problems that being at school and trying to launch yourself as a model can bring. If you are under sixteen you will need your parents' consent before you can find yourself an agent or accept work, since your father or mother will have to sign all the forms on your behalf, and officially one of them should chaperone you on any sessions for which you're booked. (In practice, a lot of fourteen- and fifteen-year-olds are more than capable of looking after themselves, and rather resent walking into a photographer's studio with Mum in tow.)

You'll find that the people you're working with make allowances for the fact that you are young and inexperienced, but they will expect you to be as professional as you can. 'I'd rather work with five-year-olds than teenagers any day,' says Julian Barry of Norrie Carr's agency. 'At least with the little ones, you know that their mothers will make sure that they're there on time, but once the teenagers start to outgrow their mother's authority they are a real head-ache. They disappear or turn up late, or forget to bring the clothes the photographer specially asked for.' The lack of professionalism among some of the girls irritates Sue James of *Fab 208* too. 'If I book a girl for a session at ten o'clock and say that I want her with curly hair, I don't expect her to arrive at ten and then spend the next forty minutes curling her hair.'

But if you are really professional, are prepared to work very hard, and to change your image when the need arises, there is no reason why your modelling career shouldn't start when you're fifteen and go on until you're in your thirties. Just think of girls like Celia Hammond, Sandra Paul, and Paulene Stone, who were top models in the mid-sixties and whose faces were still appearing regularly in magazines ten years later. Other girls give up their modelling careers when they marry, but once they're had their families and their children are growing up, they decide, in their early or mid-thirties, to take up modelling again, and some women who never had the chance to model when they were young decide in their mid-thirties that they would like to try their hand at it now.

Obviously, the women who were models do have an advantage – not only do they have invaluable experience behind them, but chances are that, since they learnt how to look after their looks when they were working, they haven't 'let themselves go'. But that's not to say that any woman who's kept her figure, has an attractive face and a strong personality, and who is prepared to train, can't have a very successful career as a more mature model. Like the younger girls, you need to learn how to walk well, although your model walk need not be quite as stylized as theirs, since there is practically no high fashion work for the more mature woman, and you also need to know how to make the best of your good points by applying make-up skilfully and subtly. Nothing is more ageing than heavily applied, obvious make-up.

Age, far from being a problem, is an asset in this particular type of modelling – one of the most successful models of all time is now in her mid-sixties. 'With the older woman,' says Patricia O'Brien of Promcat, an agency with a number of more mature models on its books, 'you do have to be careful about her face. Her bone structure has to be really very good, and if it is, then the wrinkles don't matter – in fact they are an advantage. A woman who looks at a photograph of a model has got to be able to identify with her, and if the model doesn't have any wrinkles then the woman can't do that.'

It's a mistake to try and look younger than you actually do – nothing is more ageing than 'mutton dressed as lamb'. If you look thirty-five – you must be totally honest with yourself; rose-coloured spectacles are out! – you're not going to get the jobs that the twenty-three-year-olds are going after, no matter how hard you try, so surely it's more sensible to settle for a more mature image and go after work in that market where good models are very highly sought after. 'Anyway,' says Elizabeth Woods of *Woman and Home* who runs 'Golden Corner', a regular fashion feature for the over-forties, 'a woman who strives to look younger than she is only succeeds in making you very aware of her age. A lot of women have the photographs for their index cards done with very soft focus, to take out the lines and wrinkles and make them look younger, but all that does is make me stare extra hard at the photographs to try and see just how wrinkled they really are. And anyway, I'd never book a model on the strength of an index card alone – I'd have to see her in the flesh, wrinkles and all, first.'

If your hair is going grey, then don't try to dye it back to its original colour because it can look very harsh and unnatural against an ageing skin. Either have it dyed to a colour three or four shades lighter than your natural one, or preferably let it go grey, with a little skilled help from your hairdresser if it is greying unevenly. Great beauty isn't essential – from Elizabeth Woods' point of view, nice eyes, a pleasant smile and a very strong personality that comes across to the camera, as well as the ability to relax in front of it, are far more important than outstanding good looks, though she finds it extremely difficult to find women who fit the bill. 'Either women have tended to let themselves go and their figures have spread, or if they were models when they were young, they still have the very static style of modelling that was fashionable twenty years ago, but looks all wrong now. If I use a model once and then never book her again, it's almost always because she is much too stiff in front of the camera.'

Ideally you should be about 5′ 6″, because if you're any shorter there might be problems with the length of coats, skirts and trousers, and a well-proportioned size 12, since most manufacturers' samples come in that size. If you are built on rather generous lines, then don't try to diet drastically. 'If you do,' says Patricia O'Brien, 'you'll get lots of loose skin which is extremely unattractive. Anyway, with the older woman, a size 12 or 14 figure is probably better than a size 8 because a very thin girl will probably begin to look scrawny by the time she's forty.' Apart from photographic work and the small local fashion shows put on by shops and stores, advertising photography, television commercials and film-extra work are also very lucrative sources of employment for the woman who can do character work, so the more versatile you can be with your hairstyle, your make-up and your facial expression, the more opportunities will be open to you.

When you have your index cards done, don't concentrate on 'glamorous' shots. Instead, show yourself in as many different roles as you can – a char-lady, a duchess, a prim schoolteacher, a proud grannie – so that a would-be employer can see just how versatile you are. Since you will be doing mainly advertising work, you'll need to collect together as many accessories as you can to help you create your different characters. You may find wigs are very useful here, perhaps a couple of pairs of spectacle frames in different styles too, and hats are invaluable – flowery ones for fête-opening lady mayors, stern felt ones for nannies, headscarves for charladies. It needn't cost you a fortune, either. Apart from a few smart items, most of your character props could be found at the back of your own, or friends' wardrobes, or even at jumble sales. This area of modelling is perhaps closer to acting than any other, so if you've been the leading light of the local amateur dramatic society for many years, you might find a whole new career opening up for you in your forties or even later.

For the older woman who is also a larger woman, there are opportunities for outsize modelling, providing, of course, that she is a good height – about 5′ 7″ – and that her figure is well proportioned and trim. The term 'outsize' is not only very unflattering, it is also misleading. In most people's minds it conjures up visions of 60″ hips swathed in yards and yards of beige crimplene, but in fact most outsize models are either size 14 or 16, and pad themselves out to model the larger sizes with an extra skirt underneath the one they are modelling, or a special petticoat with thin sheets of polystyrene sandwiched between two layers of fabric. Most manufacturers and photo-graphers would rather use a smaller girl – a size 14 or 16 – padded out to model the clothes, than a really large woman – a size 20 woman would have a size 20 face and size 20 arms and legs, which wouldn't look very attractive in a photograph. Obviously, you wouldn't be expected to pad out to much more than a size bigger than you actually are, or else your head, arms and legs would begin to look out of proportion with the rest of you.

Although there is some live fashion work for the larger women – stores like Harvey Nichols as well as smaller local shops put on shows two or three times a year – the majority of it is photographic, both for magazines and catalogues, and since it's unlikely that accessories will be provided, you need to have a good selection of your own.

A selection of well-fitting underwear is even more important to you than it is to a 'skinny' model – after all, there is more of you to control – so take your time when you're buying bras and girdles and make sure that they really do fit you perfectly. If you have trouble finding ready-made foundation garments, then it's worth having them made to measure. If you're wearing an ill-fitting bra, then no dress or blouse or sweater will look right on you. When you find a bra or girdle that really does fit you, it's worth investing in two or three, since manufacturers have a habit of discontinuing styles in the more unusual sizes.

There are only a comparatively small number of OS models who work regularly, so chances are that you'll know everybody on a session and the atmosphere will be very friendly, and if by any chance you don't have exactly what the photographer wants, one of the other models will be able to help you out. 'On the whole, though,' says Patricia O'Brien of Promcat, 'we find that the older women are much more professional than the young ones, and they are almost always prepared for every eventuality. They always tend to look like models, too, well-groomed and elegant, whereas the younger ones go around in jeans and T-shirts looking anything but.'

For the older woman, whether she's large or small, modelling is a marvellous 'second time around' career. Once you have established yourself, and provided, of course, that you are extremely professional about your work, there is no reason why you shouldn't carry on working till you are in your fifties or even your sixties.

Unlike the younger girls, you aren't working under the pressure that comes from knowing that if you don't 'make it' in a couple of years then the opportunity is gone, and because the competition isn't as fierce you won't feel obliged to accept every single job that comes along, so by picking and choosing you can run your career very happily in tandem with your home life.

16   Television commercials

Of all the opportunities open to models, perhaps television commercials are the most highly sought after – partly because nowhere else are you exposed to fifteen or twenty million people at the same time, and, more important, because the money is extremely good. The basic daily rate isn't much higher than the rate for photographic work, but if you are a 'featured artist' – one of the leads in the commercial – you get a percentage of your original fee every time it is shown. You only have to watch Independent Television for a couple of evenings and see how often some commercials are shown to realize that one day's work could, in the end, earn you hundreds of pounds.

Not surprisingly, the competition is extremely fierce. These days, you're not only competing with other models, you're competing against actors and actresses too. Ten or fifteen years ago, most of them thought that making commercials was beneath them and so there was a lot of scope for models playing young mums and shop assistants as well as the more glamour-ous roles, but these days members of the acting profession are a lot more realistic and there are some who earn their living exclusively from making commercials.

So in the last few years the opportunities for models have become much more limited, not only because actresses are being given the work, but also because the agreement between the commercial-producing companies and Equity, the actor's union, has been tightened up. In general terms, it states jobs in television commercials should be offered to Equity members. For some models who are already members of Equity there is no problem, but if you're a newcomer, starting out on your career, it does create difficulties. If you want to become a member of Equity, then you will have to serve the usual apprenticeship of so many weeks in a provincial repertory theatre or a summer show, even if you only want to work and model in television commercials. If you have no acting or singing or dancing ability, as many models haven't, then that isn't a real possibility either. Of course, there are ways round the problem. If a large cosmetic manufacturer, for instance, is using you in his press campaign to launch a new product, then you would be allowed to make the television commercials too, although it doesn't mean, as it would have done a few years ago, that you will automatically be granted Equity membership. The same is true if a company needs a girl with very specific qualifications – waist-length blonde hair for instance – and can't find any Equity member who's suitable. They would be allowed to use you for that commercial, but again, that doesn't mean you can apply for membership to Equity on the strength of it. For crowd work – being in the background of a pub scene, say, or one of the guests at a party – the rules aren't quite so rigid, but most directors tend to use either Equity members, or members of the Film Artists' Association, the extras' union, because they are experienced, but if they need a lot of very pretty girls they may well use models.

If you are lucky enough to be chosen for a television commercial, it's extremely unlikely that you'll be given a speaking part, since obviously an actress would be more suitable. The commercial will probably be 'shot silent', and a 'voice over' – a sort of commentary – added later, but if it actually does involve saying lines, unless your voice is outstandingly good, they will get an actress to 'dub' it afterwards, so that although your lips are moving it's her voice coming out.

'The kind of commercials for which we use models rather than actresses,' said Julia Lisney, a top casting director, 'are those that require beautiful hair or beautiful skin or beautiful hands, or for shower situations or underwear ads where you need a perfect figure – situations where the girl just has to look lovely rather than talk or act.'

Graham Baker, a director with the Moving Picture Company who've produced many prize-winning commercials, has just shot a toothpaste commercial for Dutch television. 'The brief from the client was simply to find a stunning girl with perfect teeth, beautiful fresh complexion, shiny hair, who looks bouncing with health, so we then briefed the casting director to find us models who fitted that description.' It's by no means easy to find girls with those physical qualities, but even so those qualities by themselves just aren't enough. 'The problem I find with most models,' says Graham Baker, 'is that they are trained to pose and to animate just for a frozen second in front of a stills camera, so when it comes to film or video they tend to be still and jerky because they aren't trained to be fluid and to move around.' From that point of view he finds actresses easier to work with, although he does admit that because they are used to performing, they do sometimes go 'over the top' and ruin the naturalism of a scene. 'I enjoy working with models because they aren't as complicated as actresses. If I say to a model "Open the fridge like this", then she'll do it, but an actress is likely to go into a whole big thing about the motivation of the character and wouldn't it be more in keeping if she opened the fridge with her left hand instead.'

Television commercials are big business and a lot of money is at stake, so every decision has to be approved by half a dozen different people before any action is taken. When a company is launching a new product or revamping an old one, it employs an advertising agency to handle the whole campaign – papers, magazines, posters, as well as television commercials. If the agency doesn't have a television production department of its own, it will then approach a company which specializes in making commercials to handle that side of the operation. After consultation with the client and the account executive of the advertising agency about the kind of commercial they want and about the sort of girl they're after, the director will call in a casting director, whose job is simply to get together a number of models or actresses who would be suitable for the part, from whom they can select the one they want.

This time, the director is looking for, say, bubbly brunettes of 5′ 10″ with curly hair and grey eyes, so the casting director then rings all the agencies, tells them what he is looking for and asks them to send any suitable girls along to an audition. Your agent decides that you might be just what they're looking for, although you're only 5′ 9″, and sends you along. When you arrive for the audition, you may find fifteen or twenty other curly headed brunettes already waiting, and your heart will probably sink. It's not easy, but you must keep your self-confidence intact – somebody's going to get the job, so why not you? Your agent thinks you're suitable, so you're in with a chance, and it's worth remembering that all the other girls are probably feeling just as nervous as you are. When it's finally your turn to go in, you may find yourself facing six or seven people on the other side of the table – the casting director, the director, the producer, the account executive, the client, perhaps the art director as well.

'It must be nerve-racking,' says Jean Raymond, who, as a producer of commercials with the Boase, Massimi, Pollitt Agency has sat on the other side of the table many times, 'and though we do try and make it as easy as we can for the girls it's still pretty tough on them, especially if you get a director who knows exactly what he's looking for and isn't prepared to waste time on going through the motions with a girl he knows instantly isn't right.' Do remember that nobody is getting at you personally – a lot of money is at stake and they can't afford to pick the wrong girl. And if you are "wrong", then don't take it to heart – all it means is that you don't conform to the director's or the client's ideas about that particular product, but you may be perfect for something else.

Remember, too, that the six or seven people facing you aren't all totally agreed on what they want. If you're unlucky, you could find yourself caught in the crossfire between, say, the director and the account executive. Perhaps the latter dislikes the way the former seems to be taking over control, and is determined to object to any girl the director seems to like. That is just an occupational hazard, and there is nothing you can do about it except make sure that it doesn't dent your self-confidence.

What you must try and do at an audition is to make yourself stand out from the other twenty girls they've already seen that morning, and the way to do that is not with your looks alone – after all, the other girls are equally pretty – but with your personality. Naturally you'll be nervous, but you must try very hard not to show it. The people interviewing you will understand how you feel, but if you're nervous in front of them, you're likely to be nervous in front of the camera, and that won't sell anything. Try to be as natural as possible, though if you're naturally shy and reserved then you must make an effort to be outgoing and positive, and don't come on strong. 'I've never been impressed by a big act,' says Graham Baker, 'at least I don't think I have been. If the act was so good that I didn't even realize that's what it was, then obviously that was the right girl for the job. From my point of view, the best thing for a girl to do is to come in and be herself. All the chat just wastes my time.'

Sometimes your agent may be able to tell exactly what the part is that you're auditioning for, and though obviously you wouldn't turn up in jeans with your hair in plaits if it was for a dreamy-walking-through-the-long-grass-at-dawn hairspray commercial, it doesn't always pay to dress for the part. 'I was auditioning for a chewing gum commercial yesterday and the part I was casting was a newspaper reporter,' said Graham Baker. 'One guy turned up in a loud bow-tie and a mac – his idea of what reporters dress like, whereas mine was of something much more suave, much less obvious. It doesn't really make that much difference, though. Even though somebody like that puts you off at first, you ought to be professional enough to see beyond the clothes. If he's right for the part, then he'll get it.'

For television commercials, your face – its expressiveness, not its beauty – is crucial. You may have only fifteen or twenty seconds, usually without words, to convey a mood, a state of mind, a feeling, and the only tools you have are your face and your body. After all, commercials are about selling the product you're advertising and unless you can convince the viewers that it is the softest, most delicious, most powerful, nicest smelling whatever-it-is in the world, they're not going to buy it.

Some people have more expressive faces than others, and if you're one of the unlucky ones you can improve your range of expressions by practising in front of the mirror. Even if it doesn't lead to a television commercial, the exercise is extremely good for your facial muscles.

If you do get a booking for a television commercial, you'll probably be asked to bring your own clothes if it's crowd work, and maybe even if you're a featured artist and your outfit isn't very important. It will almost certainly mean a very early start – getting up at five in the morning isn't unusual – whether it's being shot in a studio or on location. If you're only used to the comparative privacy of a photographic studio – some photographers, such as Barry Lategan, won't have anyone else in the studio apart from himself and the model – you may find a television or film studio, with twenty-five or thirty technicians around, a bit daunting at first, and you may be embarrassed at having to perform in front of so many people. Just remember that they are only interested in getting the job done as quickly and as efficiently as possible – not in laughing at you.

In photographic modelling time is money, but in television commercials, where a thirty-second film costs thousands of pounds, it is even more expensive. Make sure that you are never even two minutes late, and that you don't waste the director's time. Listen carefully to his instructions and carry them out to the full first time – every retake adds to the over-all cost, and the model who needs six takes to get the simplest thing right won't be booked again. Do use your head – if you're part of the crowd in a pub, for example, and the director doesn't give you specific instructions, then behave as you normally would in a pub, talk to the people you're with – but not too loudly or else you might drown out the featured players – or sip your drink, but don't sit and stare at the camera. These days most commercials are a slice of life, and nothing destroys the illusion of reality faster than someone staring straight into the lens.

The first time round, you'll be amazed at how long it takes to shoot a thirty-second commercial – three or four days isn't unusual – so naturally there'll be a lot of hanging about. Perhaps on the first day you were called for seven o'clock and weren't used till three, but whatever you do don't be tempted to think on the second day that you might as well not turn up till lunch-time. If the director suddenly decides to do your scene and you're not there, you'll not only lose that job, you'll never work for that director, agency, or client again. Make the most of the spare time you have – watch what's going on, see how the experienced actors and models do it, talk to the other people on the set and pick up what hints you can, but make sure that you always keep one ear open for the director's voice – nothing irritates him more than having to keep repeating his instructions or having to shout for quiet every few minutes.

You should always be prepared to work late and don't make any firm arrangements for that evening. If the commercial isn't finished at seven, you will be extremely unpopular if you insist on leaving, and force the company to spend thousands of pounds in bringing everybody back another day just to finish the last remaining shot.

Do remember that a director has an awful lot of problems – he has the client to please as well as the account executive and his own producer, the lighting, the sound, the set, the other performers to worry about besides you, so don't bother him unnecessarily. If you don't understand what he wants you to do, then by all means ask – better that than to ruin the take – but don't ask him questions simply to prove how clever you are or how eager to please. 'Actors are much more guilty of that than models,' said Graham Baker. 'They seem to need bolstering up all the time and wanting to be told how lovely they are while the models just get on with it.'

A career strictly in television commercials isn't really a viable proposition for models these days. Apart from the union difficulties, there is also the problem of over-exposure – you can only make so many commercials before your face becomes too familiar and companies don't want to use you. If you are offered a major commercial, you should think carefully before you accept it. The money will be extremely tempting, but remember there are dangers in becoming too closely associated with one product. It may be very flattering to be known everywhere as 'the Sunsoft girl', but no maker of a slimmers' bread or an aperitif will want to give Sunsoft free publicity by using you in their commercial.

Try to think of television commercials as jam – they're not your bread-and-butter, they are simply an occasional bonus.

Conclusion

By now, you should have a good idea about what it takes to become a top model, whether you're an eighteen-year-old girl, a young man in your mid-twenties, or a woman in your thirties or forties – the physical requirements, the temperament, the practical skills. But if you have decided that you want to make a career in modelling, then there is no real substitute for practical experience. And this is where a training course at one of the good modelling schools such as the London Academy of Modelling is invaluable.

During the four weeks of the course, you'll be given plenty of opportunity to practise the basic skills – you'll spend a lot of time on deportment under the stern and discerning eye of a former top model, who will keep you literally on the straight and narrow, and, equally important, in that time you'll lose your self-consciousness and get used to appearing before an audience, whether it is made up simply of your fellow-students as it will be during the course, or of friends and relatives as it is for the graduation show at the end of the course.

As well as giving you expert help and advice about everything that an aspiring model – and indeed *any* girl who wants to make the most of herself and her opportunities, both professionally and socially – needs to know, a good training course will start to instil in you the discipline, the professionalism, that is essential in modelling. At the London Academy, you are *always* expected to be on time – unpunctuality is one of the cardinal sins in modelling and the sooner you get into good habits, the better – and no excuses apart from sudden illness or perhaps a lightning transport strike are accepted. Once you've had your individual make-up lesson, you are expected to wear a full model make-up every day, and to have your nails well manicured and varnished. Not only does it give you plenty of practice in getting your make-up absolutely right, it also means you start getting used to being prepared, so that your agent can send you off to interviews or even sessions at very short notice, knowing that you're ready to step in front of a camera or a would-be employer. You're also expected to be dressed immaculately. That doesn't mean expensively. What it *does* mean is clean, well-pressed clothes, no grubby collars, or hanging hems or laddered tights. As a professional model girl, you must always look perfect from top to toe, and so, again, the sooner you start thinking and behaving that way the better.

As you've no doubt realized by now, modelling is not simply about having a pretty face. It can be a very glamorous way of life, it can be very rewarding in every sense, but it is a profession, a job of work – not a hobby or a bit of fun – with its own code, its own disciplines, and the person who gets to the top will be dedicated, very hard-working, and above all, professional.

List of model agencies

Although the fortunes of model agencies wax and wane – some close down while new ones are starting up all the time – here is a list of the best in business in 1976. Agencies do tend to specialize, so it isn't advisable to approach them 'cold'. Always seek professional advice first, either from your model school or from someone else in the fashion business, about which agencies are more likely to take you on.

LARAINE ASHTON – I.F.M
82 Park Street
London W1
629 3176

ASKEW'S
18 Bruton Place
London W1
493 0631

PETER BENISON
71 Abingdon Road
London W8
937 6575

BLACK BOYS & BLONDELL
223A Portobello Road
London W11
229 1436

BOBTON'S
36 King's Road
London SW3
584 4397

NORRIE CARR (children only)
30 Fryent Way
London NW9
204 2241

LUCIE CLAYTON
168 Brompton Road
London SW3
629 0667

COMMERCIAL TELEVISION ARTISTES
42 New Broad Street
London EC2
628 0898

DAVID AGENCY
20 Blackfriars Lane
London EC4
248 4623

FREDDIES
2 Lowndes Street
London SW1
235 8778

JULIA HUNT
48 Queens Gate Gardens
London SW1
584 4681

INTERNATIONAL MODEL AGENCY
7 Duke Street
London W1
486 3312

JCJ
100 Oxford Street
London W1
636 3982

JEAN KAYE MANAGEMENT
48 Crawford Street
London W1
724 0555

LONDON MODEL AGENCY
143 New Bond Street
London W1
629 4228

PETER LUMLEY
174 Brompton Road
London SW3
584 3747

CHERRY MARSHALL
14 Poland Street
London W1
437 8984

MODELS ONE
200 Fulham Road
London SW10
351 1195

NEVS
18 Coulson Street
London SW3
581 2295

PENNY PERSONAL MANAGEMENT
146A Brompton Road
London SW3
584 8577

PEOPLE IN PICTURES
52 Britannia Road
London SW6
736 0191

PETAL
28 Walpole Street
London SW3
730 7284

PROMCAT
12/13 Greek Street
London W1
437 3430

GAVIN L. B. ROBINSON
30 Old Bond Street
London W1
629 5231

SNAPSHOT
61 Blandford Street
London W1
486 4538

TOP MODELS
37 Percy Street
London W1
636 8771

ANNIE WALKER
44 Parkway
London NW1
485 1058

DAPHNE WEBSTER
4 Sunning Avenue
Sunningdale
Ascot, Berks
Ascot 22253

WHITTAKER ENTERPRISES
33 Brook Street
London W1
629 5849

UGLY
6 Windmill Street
London W1
636 6247

Index

Walk, 7, 69
Warbeck, David, 102
Wardrobe, 52
Way, Stephen, 28, 31
Webster, Gerda, 45
Westminster City Council, 55
Wholesale house, 9, 11
Wholesale modelling: a day in the life of
  a wholesale model, 71–5; buyers, 63, 64,
  72, 74; coat house, 63; customers, 63;
  haute couture, 67, 68; interest, 66;
  merchandise, 66; payment, 68, 69;
  prestige shows, 69; prices, 71

Wigotaifun, 29
Wigs, 32
Williams, Niké, 81, 85
Woman, 80
Woman and Home, 110
Woman's Own, 21
Woods, Elizabeth, 110
Woodward, Carolyn, 108

Yeast pack, 39
You've Gotta Have Skin, 34
Yudkin, Professor, 13, 16